Raymond Tallis was a physician and clinical scientist for nearly forty years. In addition to many books and articles on medicine and clinical science, he has published over thirty non-medical volumes of philosophy, fiction, and poetry. A Fellow of the Academy of Medical Sciences and of the Royal College of Physicians, he has honorary degrees of Doctor of Science for his contributions to medical research and of Doctor of Letters for his contributions to the humanities.

Raymond Tallis

–

THE MYSTERY OF BEING HUMAN:

God, Freedom and the NHS

To Ann Gleavens
with best wishes
Ray Tallis

nh Notting Hill Editions

Published in 2016
by Notting Hill Editions Ltd
Widworthy Barton Honiton Devon EX14 9JS

Designed by FLOK Design, Berlin, Germany
Typeset by CB editions, London

Printed and bound
by Memminger MedienCentrum, Memmingen, Germany

A CIP record for this book is available from the British Library

ISBN 978-1-910749-14-2

www.nottinghilleditions.com

Dedicated to members of Stockport NHS Watch.
Wonderful friends. Tireless defenders of the NHS.
Good people in wicked times.

Contents

– Preface –

The very virtues of the essay form may count against it. Brevity is seen as the mark of slightness and variety translates into lack of sustained purpose. The genre is, it seems, one of chamber pieces, even bagatelles, while truly serious writers aim at symphonies and operas: the fat novel, the weighty treatise, the book-length biography.

We can, of course, turn this on its head. Brevity, after all, is worn as a badge of honour by short story writers and lyric poets who are praised for packing much into small spaces. As for variety, we admire books of verse where death, a butterfly, an air-blue gown, and a rose-red sunset occupy successive pages, populated by perhaps a dozen lines offset from the chatter of the garrulous world by a moat of silence signified by wide margins. Collections of short fictions that introduce us to new characters, places, and stories at intervals of only a few pages win praise for the versatility and breadth of sympathy of the author. The essay, a genre with porous boundaries, equally at ease with argument, story-telling and reportage, with careful analysis and lyrical celebration, should surely not be ashamed of itself.

Collections of essays may also seem rather too obviously collected, rounding up items that have in common only the fact that they issued from the same writer and are (perhaps) looking for a second home. They are 'occasional' and the occasion may have passed. There is a more interesting truth hereabouts. Georg Christoph Lichtenberg spoke of his own philosophy as being 'a doctrine of scattered occasions'. A brilliant scientist and free-ranging thinker, he gathered his philosophical thoughts in scrapbooks, and they never amounted to a system. He felt that there was something irreducibly multiple, fragmented, episodic, accidental in the thoughts of even the most focussed thinker. Lichtenberg was greatly admired by Ludwig Wittgenstein and would doubtless have approved of the latter's description of his own unfinished posthumous *Philosophical Investigations* as 'an album of sketches'.

Indeed, we might go on to the front foot and argue that length – or lack of it – respects the attention span of the reader or, if that too can be turned on its head, the reading span. The essay is a mind-portable form. The apparent unity and sustained flow of the novel, the big biography, or the treatise is not replicated in the experience of their readers. Reading is scattered through readings. A novel is dipped into on the toilet, on a tube train between stops, on the edge of sleep, in a doctor's surgery when the news of a blood test is awaited. Its characters' lives have to negotiate the torrent of experiences that is the reader's life.

Among my publications is a 1,000-page trilogy on human consciousness, and a forthcoming treatise *Of Time and Lamentation: Reflections on Transience* at approximately eight hundred pages betrays that I am not a consistent advocate of the short form. But I am aware that the apparent unity and coherence of even the most tightly argued work, however scrupulous, rigorous, and comprehensive in its intention, is more appearance than reality. The boundaries are the result of decisions that are external to the matter; and within those boundaries there are gaps, elisions, and disconnections. The essay, which bears its provisional nature and incompleteness on its sleeve, is therefore more honest in this regard. It is an antidote to the fantasy of gathering the world up in one sustained glance: it respects the irreducible variousness of things, and the incompleteness of thought. The latter is intrinsically centrifugal, expressed in the tension between the processes of reflection, which have no natural boundaries, and its publishable products that have a clear beginning and end.

In short, the essay is an appropriate form for the humanism that I have been seeking to express for several decades often at great length. The pieces that follow are for the most part philosophical but they are relatively unbuttoned, though the philosophical novice may sometimes find them demanding. While larger ideas dominate over small observations, there is no pretence to a definitive treatment of the topics they address. The wonderfully witty philosopher J. L. Austin offered a footnote to one of the last papers he gave before his premature death:

I dreamed a line that would make a motto for a sober philosophy: '*Neither a be-all nor an end-all be*'.

It is in the spirit of this sentiment that these philosophical essays are offered to the reader. And, what is more, there is a hidden nerve of association connecting the pieces, so the occasions of their non-doctrine are not entirely scattered.

This is hinted at in the opening essay, 'Humanity: Neither God's Work nor a Piece of Nature', which is the closest I can manage to a mission statement: namely, to try to characterise a secular humanism that, while distancing itself from religious belief, does not merely dismiss something that (for good or ill) has been central to our humanity. Nor does it subscribe to a naturalism that sees us as ultimately explicable by biological science. The essay – and, less explicitly, its successors – is a non-strident Prologue to a humanism that celebrates the infinite complexity of beings who are unique in unique ways; who are offset from nature as well as a part of it; and who are able to wake out of themselves and their organic condition, even to the point of believing in God and Eternity. Consistent with its non-stridency is what I hope is a balanced view of the impact on humanity of religious belief.

This approach to our humanity is explored in 'On Being Thanked by a Paper Bag' which reflects on the irreducible complexity of human consciousness, prompted by the everyday experience referred to in the title. A belief in our freedom – the cornerstone of human dignity – is defended in the third essay 'How on Earth Can We Be Free?'

Freedom is, however, shaped and constrained by our circumstances. For this reason, the piece that follows, 'Lord Howe's Wicked Dream: A Report from an Undeveloping Country' is not as out of place as it may seem in a book of largely philosophical essays. Illness makes it more difficult to philosophise and death makes it impossible. Anyone who is interested in sharing philosophical ideas with their fellow citizens should take an interest in their health. This is particularly true if, as in my own case, he spent most of his adult life working as a doctor. The essay exposes a recent assault on an institution, the NHS, and the values that have created and sustained it. Behind this is a wider regression towards barbarity. It is expressed in policies that have no electoral mandate, eating away at the foundations of the postwar settlement driven by an institutionally corrupt political class. Their spokespersons sound as if butter would not melt in their mouths, as they gas the hopes of the poorest and most vulnerable.

If there is a link between the polemic of this fourth essay and the argument of its successor – '"All

Is Number": Mathematics, Reality and the Madness of Max Tegmark' – it is in the analogy between the reduction of values to prices in neo-liberal economics and of quality to quantities in physical science and the increasingly prevalent idea that the universe and the human world boils down to numbers.

In accordance with the humanist spirit of the opening essay, the final piece considers the significance that the ideas of God and Eternity may have for an infidel. It is motivated by the belief that escaping from religion is only the beginning, not the end, of a quest for deeper understanding of what we are. Humanity, after all, is a work in progress and truly humanist thought – that begins with questions and ends with questions – should reflect this.

– Humanity: Neither
God's Work nor a Piece of Nature –

I have called myself an atheist since I was a teenager. In recent years, however, I have noticed a tendency, particularly when on the podium, to describe myself as 'a secular humanist'. This still sometimes seems to be a borrowed coat that is many sizes too large for my day-to-day existence. Religious believers probably feel the same when they classify the self that runs for buses, supports Manchester United, and waits impatiently to be served at the bar, as 'Catholic' or 'Anglican' or whatever.

My preference has to do with something believers point out with a regularity that I am inclined to call monotonous: namely, that 'atheism' is a negative term, a position defined merely by that which it opposes, like a vacuum by its non-vacuous surroundings. Being a 'Not-ist' doesn't sound very fulfilling and most certainly does little justice to the philosophical sentiments that infuse the life and thought of the rich god-free stream of humanism.

More importantly, much atheist thought is, usually unintentionally, anti-humanist. It would be unfair and distracting to single out individual thinkers; sufficient to note that some of the most prominent theocides not only virulently reject the contribution that religious belief has made to the development of human culture but also espouse a naturalistic, and hence impoverished, understanding of humanity. The latter has been insufficiently noticed but it is a particular bugbear of mine. I'll come to this presently, but first a glance at the more conventional case that humanists mount against religion: a look at the dark side.

It may seem scarcely necessary to preach an anti-sermon on the frequently malign role religion has played in human affairs. If I add my footprints to this well-trodden territory, it is because I would not wish you to think that I underestimate the importance of those things that rouse the passion of some of the most prominent contemporary atheists. I am as conscious as they of how religion has been used to justify atrocious behaviour in private and public life, from the domestic sphere to international politics, from the abuse of children to wars of conquest. You don't have to have much knowledge of history to be aware of the abominations inflicted on human beings in its name: unspeakably bloody confessional wars – including the current conflicts in the Middle East that are setting Sunni against Shia and Islam against Christianity and everybody against everyone else; sectarian cruelty and injustice; the crushing of the life chances of women (and the destructive obsession that priests have with what goes into and comes out of the female pelvis, expressed in female genital mutilation and the control of fertility);

and a cynical and opportunistic alignment with temporal powers in maintaining an unjust *status quo* that benefits the few at the top of the heap and keeps the many at the bottom.

With admirable exceptions, organised religion is intrinsically conservative, putting power behind the rich and powerful and only its rhetoric behind the poor and powerless. Even where churches and mosques and temples have not directly sponsored savagery, they have often found it prudent to remain silent and to avert their gaze when it is happening. God's representative in the Vatican did not make too much of a fuss over the Holocaust. The Holy See also chose not to see in Croatia where, out of ecclesiastical self-interest, that vilest of war criminals Ante Pavelic was supported when he was in power and protected when he fell. In Rwanda in 1994, the Catholic hierarchy eagerly joined in the slaughter and their churches were auxiliary killing fields. In many cases, wickedness is normalised by the authority of priests and unquestioning obedience demanded of believers, justifying the extermination of unbelievers, or those whose very existence, because they worship the wrong gods or the right God in the wrong way, must be an offence to the Almighty.

Even the gentlest of divine beings, Jesus Christ, warned that those who did not help Him would be cursed and sent into 'eternal fire' (Matthew 25:41); and the Gospel's bringer of peace and joy on a humble donkey could turn into a better mounted mass killer in the Book of Revelation. Doctrines in which Peace, Love, Mercy and Forgiveness are prominent are not infrequently promulgated with the aid of the sword, boiling oil, and the hangman's noose.

God's commitment to savagery pops up in the most surprising places. At a recent concert in a local church, the choir (made up of perfectly normal and seemingly decent individuals), lustily proclaimed – to Handel's gorgeous music – that The Lord would 'judge among the heathen, he shall fill the place with dead bodies: he shall wound the heads over many countries' (Psalm 110.) Religiously justified wickedness, it appears, is not merely episodic and accidental but systemic.

Even allowing for the fact that people are perfectly capable of treating each other badly, and being ego-centric, aggressive or cruel, without the assistance of religious belief, it is arguable that doctrinal loyalties amplify tribal antipathies. They furnish transcenden-tal justification for unimaginable nastiness, enabling the victims, being heathens, infidels, followers of false gods, or whatever, to be seen as deserving of their horrible fate.

For some critics of religion, its propensity to fo-ment or exacerbate conflict goes to its very heart. This is the burden of the French *philosophe* Denis Diderot's anguished fable:

A man had been betrayed by his children, his wife and his friends. Treacherous partners had destroyed his fortune and made him destitute. Filled with hatred and deep contempt for the human race, he left society and took refuge in a solitary cavern. There, pressing his fists into his eyes, and planning revenge proportionate to his bitterness, he said: 'Monsters! What shall I do to punish their acts of injustice and make them as wretched as they deserve? Ah, were it but possible . . . to put into their heads an illusion, which they would think more important than their own lives, on which they could never agree with each other . . .' At that moment, he rushed out of the cavern crying 'God! God!' Countless echoes all around him repeated 'God! God!' The terrifying name was carried from pole to pole and everywhere it was heard with astonishment. Men at first fell down to worship, then they rose, asked questions, argued, became embittered, cursed one another, hated one another, and cut one another's throats. Thus was the deadly wish of the hater of mankind fulfilled. For such has been the past history, and such is the future of a being who is as important as he is incomprehensible.

– *Additions aux Pensées Philosophiques,* 1770

The potential for religious violence within cultures is proportionate to the passion with which the convictions are held, the extent to which the religions are institutionalised, and the degree to which those institutions not only draw authority, but also power, from the domestic, civic, and political worlds in which they are located. A dogmatic religion expressed in a theocracy is the almost perfect recipe for human unhappiness. Beheading, behanding, and the generous use of the lash for apostasy, for the crime of resisting marital rape, for minor acts of theft, are imaginable only where religions dominate the spaces that should be occupied by civil society.

Behind the role of religions as an organiser and amplifier of earthly spite, vindictiveness, and hatred, there is, some have argued, a deeper source of the evils it has facilitated. The Islamic State of Iraq and Syria, better known as ISIS, has been described as a death cult – which it most certainly is – but it is scarcely unique in this respect. The cult of death is implicit in many, perhaps all, religions. The devaluation of ordinary life is a correlative of the over-valuation of a putative life on the far side of death. This has wider consequences even than the slaughter of the innocents – or the retributive extermination of those deemed guilty, to keep the cycle of violence in motion: it may inhibit improvements that will make life this side of the grave more bearable for the hungry, the destitute, the downtrodden. The duty to mitigate suffering is less of a priority when a tragic sense of life, of helplessness against the will of God, and the cult of a life beyond life, and of sacrifice in this one, prevails. Cynics will note that leaders of churches and mosques and temples have not always hesitated to ameliorate the tragedy of life in their own case and have availed themselves of the technological benefits that have come from decidedly secular sciences of which they may disapprove.

Humanism, by contrast is content to let the afterlife, if there is one, look after itself. This, perhaps more than any conflict over specific matters such as the origin of the universe, makes religion and science – with the latter's commitment to advancing knowledge and, through technological advance and hence improving the lot of humanity – natural antagonists. Admittedly, many great scientists were deeply religious and indeed were inspired by their religious beliefs in the development of their ideas. Some historians of science have argued that the search for laws of nature is an expression of intuition of a unified world created by a Divine Intelligence. Certainly, the prominence given to the emblematic collision between Galileo and the Catholic church, or the opposition of many religious groups to Darwinism, has sometimes distorted the often amicable relationship between men of science and men of God, and between religious and scientific modes of understanding. We are all too familiar with fundamentalist Islamists using cutting edge communication systems, most prominently 21st-century social media, to spread their ancient message of an all-powerful deity whose will determines all that happens in the world. This cognitive inconsistency goes beyond the quaint dissonance that Jean-Paul Sartre registered when he pronounced a nun on a motor scooter as being as surreal an object as Merle Oppenheimer's celebrated furlined tea cups and marble sugar cubes.

Nevertheless, there is a real antagonism of fundamental cognitive attitudes. Science begins – and ends – with questions and religion begins – and ends – with answers; one deals in actively cultivated uncertainties and the other tries to find a resting place in dogma. One is progressive and indeed makes progress and the other, as the world outside of its citadel advances around it, seems to regress, seeking the certainties of a past whose iniquities are often forgotten.

To spell out the contrast in this simple way is to overlook a dogmatic tendency in science and also the value placed on 'honest doubt' in life histories of the Great Believers and the ordinary faithful alike – to be rather starry-eyed about the former and to dismiss the latter. Nevertheless, dogmas in science are (by the timescale of religion) soon overthrown and they are defeated not by the sword but by data. And although the spiritual pilgrim is allowed agonies of doubt, they are permitted only *en route* back to the beliefs that were doubted.

Thus the standard humanist case for the prosecution. It is, of course, grossly simplistic and it is pitched at the level of generalisation where half-truths can stand in for the whole truth. For this reason, I don't think it is possible to draw unassailable conclusions about the net moral, cognitive and material influence of religious belief. We cannot run the course of history twice – once with and once without religion – to determine whether religion has made us treat each other worse or even whether it has been an obstacle in other ways to human progress against suffering. In short, we simply do not know whether, notwithstanding the documented horrors, religion is an overall force for evil. We lack the God's eye view necessary to arrive at a true judgement as to the ratio of comfort to terror, kindness to nastiness, prompted by the promises of religion. There will, anyway, be no single answer encompassing different religions, cultures, nations, and historical periods. We should not forget, moreover, that Diderot's fable *begins* with wickedness, before the idea of God was put into circulation. Though religious doctrines have proved remarkably effective at organising, inflaming and sustaining hostilities, the propensity for grand-scale violence against 'the other' can be sustained without reference to conflicting ideas of God.

Apologists have also pointed to the moral codes that have been inculcated by religions and which, they say, have distanced us from the dog-eat-dog ethos of most of the other representatives of the animal kingdom. At the heart of many religions is the golden rule to treat others as you would wish yourself to be treated, if only because, they like you are God's children, made in his image, and beloved of Him. And there is the long history of religiously inspired charities, almshouses, hospitals, and asylums, some of which were run on humane principles not evident elsewhere in society. The liberal values we secular humanists hold dear are in part the children of the monotheism, and the idea of a just (though irritable) God, particularly associated with Judaism and Christianity.

It is not impossible therefore that a god-free, priest-free history, unfolding in the absence of the sacred and the profane and of the afterlife to structure our thinking about the world, might have been even more bloody and cruel. As Dostoevsky put into the mouth of Ivan Karamazov in *The Brothers Karamazov*: 'If God does not exist, then everything is permitted'. One translation of this thought is that a godless universe will be one without justice or a tendency to goodness. In the absence of the constraints on our behaviour applied by the idea of a law-giving God who will judge us and punish or reward us in an afterlife according to our deserts, it is argued, we will live an amoral existence entirely devoted to maximising our own pleasures; that what we ought to do will be replaced by what we can get away with.

Philip Zuckerman, however, has pointed out that the most godless or god-free societies in history – Denmark and Sweden – are the happiest and have the lowest crime and disorder rate and an often admirable record of concern for world affairs. The contrast between godless Copenhagen and Stockholm and devout Beirut, Baghdad, and Belfast could not be greater. Steven Pinker's mighty 1,000-page *The Better Angels of Our Nature* has noted a general trend towards a diminution of violence, of petty bad behaviour, and an increased regard for the welfare of an ever-widening circle of our fellow human beings in recent centuries at a time of increasing secularisation, notwithstanding intermittent catastrophic regressions to barbarity.

But even this is not decisive. There are many other historical, political, geographical differences between countries secularists would characterise as blessed with atheism and those cursed by religion. And the trends observed by Pinker have been contested. So we still cannot identify the distinctive contribution of religion to good behaviour or bad. Religious hatred may simply be a manifestation of hatred that has other causes. Perhaps we have not been godless long enough to know how things will unfold in future. How will it look after a thousand rather than a mere couple of hundred years of progressive secularisation? It is impossible to know.

There is, however, another source of reassurance that a humanist world would not necessarily be an amoral one. It comes from something that appears to be central to our human nature and unique to humans among living beings. It is a special kind of hunger for others, and linked with this, a hunger to think well of ourselves through being thought well of by others. It was the German philosopher G. W. F. Hegel who placed this at the centre of his philosophy.

All animals have appetites – for food, drink, sex, and so on; but the human person, being self-conscious, has a special kind of appetite: an appetite to engage the self-consciousness of others. One manifestation of this is that we judge and value ourselves as we are judged and valued by others. And it is important that those by whom we are judged and valued are free agents. There is no satisfaction in being worshipped, admired, loved by those who are enslaved or deceived by us. What we long for is an acknowledgement by equals. This is the profound existential origin of our desire for goodness, integrity, justified self-satisfaction, for the impulse towards altruism – that may, of course, not extend far beyond our own circle. It reaches to the heart of our sense of what we are. Hence the otherwise unexplained joy of doing good, in which we deny ourselves things in order that others may have them. And hence, too, hypocrisy which is, as La Rochefoucauld said, the tribute that vice pays to virtue: it shows by default how deeply rooted is our morality.

It would seem, therefore, that there are resources within human nature that will sustain the moral codes necessary for us to live peaceably and supportively together and that they are nourished by a profound sense of what we are and what gives meaning to our lives, even though they are rather intermittently deployed. Thinking this way suggests how we might turn the assumption that morality is rooted in religion on its head and assert that religion is rooted, at least in part, in morality. The ethical aspects of religion have grown out of our sense of our need for others: what we interpret as a love of God is actually our love of other humans. And the sense of God as a judge may well be the transcendental projection of our fellows as judges, of the collective viewpoint of others, beyond our life.

This upside down view of the relationship between religion and morality is scarcely original. It is most famously associated with Ludwig Feuerbach but there are glimpses of it in pre-Socratic philosophy. I resurrect it to suggest that Ivan Karamazov may not have been a very good sociologist of the human heart. The appeal to a transcendental underpinning for our moral codes – that want to believe that they are authorised by God – shows how deep the notion of a moral code runs in us. Secular humanists should therefore be reassured by the apparent need we seem to have to ground our morality in something that is wider, deeper, and longer-lasting than our own lives and the transient worlds in which we live.

Even if we remain undecided (as we should) as to the overall impact of religion throughout history, it is clear at the present time that conflicting religious convictions are potentially damaging for our capacity to live together on a planet which is not only overcrowded but also in which its inhabitants are intensely aware of each other. My espousal of atheism in Paris is an implicit critique of the way you worship your God in Beirut – indeed it is close to insulting and insults can nowadays be exchanged between one culture and another at the speed of light.

None of this licenses seeing religion as simply a nightmare from which humanity will one day awake. Even less should it be dismissed as mistaken or primitive or bad science. Better to acknowledge that, while science is the major cultural fact of our age, religion has been the major cultural fact of previous ages. We will not begin to understand what we are unless we know and try to imagine what we have been. Any attempt to do justice to our humanity, therefore, must take into account religious beliefs: to dismiss something profound and constant in our humanity would be a strange attitude for a humanist. A true humanism will endeavour to engage with religious beliefs and respect them – though it will not feel obliged to endorse them and will not refrain from criticising any obstacle they present to human flourishing. For humanists, too, are benefactors of a religious heritage. Iconic art, renaissance polyphony, and cathedrals – mighty works of *homo religiosus* – should feed into our sense of the mysterious creatures we are. The myths that nourished us in the past, therefore, must not be seen merely as a waning asset that will have diminishing meaning as religion fades to a distant memory. They belong to man at his most profound.

Nor does it follow from what has been said about the cultural heritage that humanists ought to embrace one religion or another by an act of will. There are two hundred or more on offer and, unless you are swept towards one or other of them by the accident of birth or powerful cultural currents, the exercise of belief will seem to require an arbitrary choice. As Anthony Kenny, philosopher and erstwhile priest, has pointed out, 'The creeds of the major religions are mutually contradictory, so that the one thing we know for certain about religion is that if any religion is true, then most religions are false.' An ecumenical synthesis that embraced the Wee Frees and Zoroastrianism by trying to find the highest common factor in all creeds would be hard pressed to have any content. Humanism will be equidistant from the faiths and rituals of druids and deacons, prelates and pagans.

Equally, it would be wrong to espouse a low-cost sentimentality about religions of the past, to forget the barbarity that they licensed, to overlook the child terrorised by the prospect of eternal damnation, the woman helpless against psychological, physical, and sexual abuse, the lost cognitive opportunity-cost of indoctrination, the inculcation of servility, and the sickening, widespread violence committed in the name of God and those who speak for Him. The overwhelming beauty of a cathedral filled with spine-tingling music should not distract us from the fact that it was built by brutally treated serfs whose disposable lives anticipated that seen today in the construction of vanity projects for billionaires, such as a stadium in Qatar, where the shallow religion of sport may be practised.

Continued insistence on the universal competence of science will serve only to undermine the credibility of science as a whole. The ultimate outcome will be an increase in radical scepticism that questions the ability of science to address even the questions within its sphere of competence. One longs for a new Enlightenment to puncture the pretensions of this latest superstition.

    — Austin Hughes 'The Folly of Scientism'.

Humanism has other, less prominent adversaries. Among them is indifference to large ideas, often dictated by the unrelenting treadmill of work and pleasure that leaves many lives largely unexamined, or the result of a distractibility that tears human consciousness into pieces too small to house sustained reflection, and too shallow to accommodate thought that challenges itself. Sleep is ubiquitous and it finds a thousand ways of extinguishing wakefulness. Even when we are spared the unchosen engulfments of hunger, pain, and privation that mark the lives of those who live in subsistence economies, we still manage to lose ourselves: in preoccupations that hide the mystery, miracle, and misery of our condition, in the pastimes, hobbies, occupations available 24/7 in our electronic world.

There is, however, another, more specifically intellectual enemy of humanism that must be confronted not because it has the potentially malign power of organised religion (though seemingly harmless puppies sometimes grow up to be Rottweilers) but because it is espoused by many influential writers who consider themselves humanists. I am referring to naturalism that sees us as mere animals, and animals as living matter that boils down to molecular machines.

Naturalism can take the form of the kind of brutal

physicalism expressed by Nobel Prize-winning physicist Steven Weinberg:

All the explanatory arrows point downwards from societies to people, to organs, to cells, to biochemistry, to chemistry, and ultimately to physics. Societies are explained by people, people by organs, organs by cells, cells by biochemistry, biochemistry by chemistry, and chemistry by physics.

For explanation read 'understanding'. A less extreme form of scientism is from E. O. Wilson. He is the prophet of 'consilience' – the linking together of the principles and methods of different disciplines in pursuit of an overarching theory:

the humanities, ranging from philosophy and history to moral reasoning, comparative religion, and interpretation of the arts, will draw closer to the sciences and partly fuse with them.

This is not as even-handed as it sounds because the fusion that Wilson envisages is one that takes place not in some neutral territory but in the homeland of science.

Given that natural science is possibly mankind's greatest cognitive glory and given also that its impact in transforming our lives is our greatest collective achievement, is it not entirely consistent with humanism that we should look to science to understand ourselves? The answer is no – because natural science has flourished by marginalising something central to our humanity. It is essentially objective, quantitative and general, focussing on law-governed mechanisms. By contrast, our humanity is defined by subjective, qualitative, individual experience characterised by agency.

At the heart of science is measurement and getting the human subject, with his or her prejudices, parochial viewpoints, and values, out of the way. Galileo famously said that the book of nature was written in the language of mathematics. Quantities – size, shape, and number are primary – and those experiences that colour them in – colour, smell, taste etc. – are merely secondary. As for meanings and values, pains and pleasures, they are yet more marginal – mere tertiary qualities. The consequences of this mode of thought are vast, as historian of science E. A. Burtt pointed out:

In the course of translating this distinction of primary and secondary into terms suited to the new mathematical interpretation of nature, *we have the first stage in the reading of man quite out of the real and primary realm.*

As natural science becomes more fundamental and its laws more general, so subjective experience and qualities are squeezed more completely out of its account of the world. Everyday objects – tables and chairs and rocks and trees – disintegrate into clouds of atoms and, in the quantum gaze, become even more elusive. We enter an upside down world in which pain, fear, and the colour yellow are deemed unreal compared with the quantum vacuum whose restlessness is said to have blasted the universe into existence.

This physicalist world picture is entirely unfitted to create a portrait of ourselves, even less to address, or give answers to, the fundamental existential and metaphysical questions that life presents to us. The assumptions that to know the world is to see it in terms of its most fundamental physical laws as they apply to its most basic constituents, that (mathematical) physics is the supreme form of knowledge, and that nothing that lies outside the ken of physics is real, lead to Weinberg's unsurprising conclusion that the world is a rather cheerless place:

The more we know of the universe, the more meaningless it appears.

If you removed meaning at the outset of your inquiry, you shouldn't be surprised if you don't find it at the end. Specifically, human life will most definitely seem void of meaning if you empty meaning out of our humanity by dissolving it into a world picture that has no space for significance, purpose, and value.

There are less radical forms of naturalistic nihilism. For example, there are writers who feel that the rejection of religious belief requires them to deny human uniqueness. The human person they argue, is really an animal organism and, given that we are identical with our evolved brains that are wired into the material world, we lack free will. Such scientism lies behind what I have called 'Darwinitis' (not Darwinism, which is fine) and 'Neuromania'. Darwinitis claims that Darwinism explains not only the origin of the organism *H. sapiens* but also the human person. According to Neuromania we are our brains and the only way to advance our understanding of ourselves is through peering into the darkness of our skulls and looking at neural activity. Neuromania fails to grasp that the brain is the beginning and not the end of the story of humanity. Our brains are our entrance tickets into the theatre of human life but the drama in which we participate is forged in the community of minds to which our brains give us access.

These scientific fantasies have exercised me somewhat over the years because they can lead to this kind of view expressed by the celebrity misanthrope John Gray, who asserts in *Straw Dogs* that we are not particularly special: 'human life has no more meaning than that of a slime mould'; 'man is only one of many species and not obviously worth preserving'.

Those with religious beliefs may now be understandably thinking: 'I told you so. If you remove the religious basis for our self-understanding, you will empty the world of meaning and significance. Man will become an animal or a piece of matter in a material world'.

Actually, this doesn't follow. It is possible to entertain a view of humanity that avoids *both* supernatural explanations of what we are, according to which we are handmade by God, and a naturalism that says we are just another part of the animal kingdom, of nature, or of the material world. My kind of humanism keeps its eyes sufficiently open to notice what is in front of its nose. It acknowledges that humankind is like nothing else in the living world or indeed the universe. We are neither spirits entirely divorced from the natural, material world nor a heap of atoms.

It is not mere vanity to think that we are fundamentally different from slime mould. After all, unlike the latter, we have the concept of 'slime mould'. More importantly, we import into, or discover meaning in, the world when we value ourselves and, crucially, each other. The fact that we are minute compared with the known universe makes us more, not less, significant. As Marcello Gleiser has put it in 'Meaning in a Silent Universe', 'Our significance should not be measured by our size relative to the rest of the cosmos, but rather by how different we are from everything else in it'.

Much of my own writing has been committed to making this more visible. I have attempted to describe the distance between ourselves and the animal kingdom and speculated on the biological means by which we ultimately escaped the biological prescriptions that define the lives of other animals and became complex selves that live their lives rather than organisms that merely suffer or endure them; by which we slipped the constraints of our organic bodies and stepped into a distinctly human realm, to an important degree off-set from nature. In that domain, uniquely, we guide, justify, and excuse our behaviour according to general and abstract principles; create cities, laws, institutions; frame our individual lives within a shared history; and (sometimes) inquire into the order of things and the patterns of causation and physical laws that seem to underpin that order. Unlike stones, trees, frogs, and chimpanzees, we even entertain theories about our own nature.

These phenomena, albeit profound and complex and pervasive, are mere surface manifestations or symptoms of something even more profound, complex and pervasive: that we are *explicit* animals living out shared and individual narratives, conscious of ourselves, of others and of the material world and its intrinsic existence and properties in a way that no other animal is. V. S. Ramachandran, a neuroscientist, and himself inclined from time to time to Neuromania, surely spoke truly when he asserted that 'Humanity transcends apehood to the same degree by which life transcends mundane chemistry and physics'.

So we must set aside naturalism as if it were the only alternative to religion, and the mistaken assumption that natural science will eventually reveal our true nature; that the last word about us will be uttered by ladies and gentleman in white coats, as they were once spoken by men in priestly robes.

—

Humanism has many facets and, indeed, the term has an essential vagueness that cannot be eliminated since it has evolved through history and has often been defined against other positions. At the heart of humanism is a faith in humanity to sort out its own affairs, to set its own goals. It will be on the side of free scientific inquiry but not scientism. It will (of course) respect the freedom of individuals to live the life that they choose to live so long as it does not harm others. It embraces the golden rule, shared with the best of religious belief, that one should treat others as one would wish to be treated. It lays upon all who are capable of it the duty to contribute to the goal of making it possible for men and women to live free of fear, fetters, oppression, and destitution.

To say this is to risk reducing humanism to a set of pious wishes and platitudes. And I am aware that the future of humanity is uncertain. The very fact that *L'homme infiniment surpasse l'homme* means we could be on the road to self-destruction, though the pessimistic assumption that we are could itself be self-fulfilling. Humanism must draw on religion and science but not fall uncritically under the spell of either. Somewhere in the space between supernaturalism and naturalism we shall find ourselves.

The humanist challenge to make a full, true, and just sense of ourselves – to construct a viewpoint from which we will see human life in all its strangeness, sorrow, and glory – remains daunting. Any story we tell about human life must try to reconcile our knowledge of the physical world with the very different sense we make of ourselves individually and at different collective levels, and at the same time reserve a space for the luminous darkness that comes from a justified sense of wonder. Accepting that we are neither handmade by God nor just a piece of nature is therefore only a start. Armed to the teeth against our own preconceptions and habits of thought, we need to think long and hard if we are ever to form an image of ourselves that does justice to our extra-natural nature.

Humanism, a collective journey of mankind, has a long way to go.

2

– On Being Thanked by a Paper Bag –

Reflections on Human Consciousness

O n the way out of a shop a little while back, I looked at the bag containing my purchases. 'Thank you,' it said. 'Please call again.' This warm invitation could not have been anticipated from my experience over the previous few minutes which (speaking off the record) had not given a strong impression that my custom had been valued.

A few days later, I was on a train and after the routine requests to 'be alert' and 'to report any suspicious items or behaviour' there was a further announcement, preceded by earwax-melting ding dongs, to the effect that the train would arrive late. There followed a beautifully crafted and sincere-sounding apology for 'this delay and for any inconvenience caused'. I suspected the recording had been triggered by a software programme designed to detect a discrepancy between the actual and the scheduled location of the train. Any human consciousness involved in the apology – in the boardroom of Virgin trains, in their departments of engineering and customer care – had long switched to other things.

These instances of automated courtesy of machine-generated manners reminded me of how often we are addressed by words uprooted from any conscious individual or even identifiable source; by announcements-without-enunciators apologising, exhorting, and ordering us about. Once you notice it, you see and hear it everywhere. The bottle out of which I drink beer advises me to 'drink sensibly' (rather than, say, to get wasted and fall over), the can of Zero Calories pop congratulates me on the healthy choice I have made. Wrappings warn me not to misuse their contents and invite me to dispose of themselves tidily. Notices on the grass forbid me to walk on the turf upon which they are elevated on their slim wooden legs. Doormats and towns welcome me – doormats unconditionally, towns if I drive carefully. Buses have apologies ('Sorry. Out of Service') printed on their foreheads. Phone-hold music is interrupted at regular intervals by the reassurance that 'Your call is valuable to us' and thanking me for my patience. My mobile wishes me 'Goodbye' when I switch it off. Notices even warn me against 'Standing forward of this notice' – that is, of themselves.

These examples of the printed and pre-recorded discourse that assails us constantly are instances of what the philosopher J. L. Austin called 'performatives'. Performatives are utterances that do not merely state something true or false about the world but perform that of which they speak – for example, promises. Austin eventually concluded that *all* utterances are performatives of a sort or 'illocutionary acts' – even apparent statements of fact. When I state a fact, I perform the speech act of 'informing'.

His original examples of performatives, however, were distinguished by the way they wore their status as *acts* on their sleeves. Uttering the sentence 'I apologise' doesn't merely report an ongoing apology but actually performs it. Of course, as even small children know, there are ways of saying 'I apologise' in such a manner that the performative can 'unperform' itself. 'All right, I apologise if you insist' does the opposite of what it says. And 'Thanks *a bunch*!' unthanks a bunch and a half.

Nevertheless, explicit performatives seem to have a personal warrant, an existential payload that mere 'informatives' asserting something that may or may not be the case, don't. Which is why delegating them to insentient machines and plebs such as paper bags seems especially noteworthy, and why the printed gratitude of the paper bag teased me somewhat. 'Manners makyth machine' – to vary that famous motto of the founder of Winchester College – is distinctly odd. At any rate, when I am being a philosopher and not wasting the gift of life in being a Grumpy Old Man, I find them intriguing. For they are a rather exotic expression of our human capacity for 'exographic storage' of elements whose primary home is human consciousness.

And so I arrive at my theme.

GLANCES AT HUMAN CONSCIOUSNESS

Or not quite. I shall park up 'exographic storage' for a while and step back to examine what I have just called 'human consciousness'. It is far too large and nebulous a theme to be wrapped up in a flurry of paragraphs. Still, I can't resist making a few, rather general comments, directed at those who claim that consciousness is the sort of stuff we can see when we look at brains with hi-tech scans or that there is no fundamental difference between human consciousness and the kind of awareness enjoyed by animals, notably our nearest primate kin. The latter is a very popular fallacy and it goes under many names: sociobiology and evolutionary psychology are two of the commonest.

One way of dealing with this fallacy is to look at our actual behaviour and how remote it is from what you see when you examine other primates. When you do, you will very quickly be struck by the extent to which we humans turn the tables on the biological givens and make them serve distinctly human, or cultural purposes. I could talk about the transformation of feeding into dining, learning into education, or the expression of the mating instinct in marriage.

Let me, however, illustrate this with a rather humble example: the use (or more precisely misuse) of saliva whose multiplicity of primary, biological functions need not detain us here. We usually find others'

saliva rather repulsive for very complex as well as obvious reasons. Even our own saliva can be rather unattractive. Think about filling a glass with your own
spit. Would you fancy drinking it in half an hour's
time? All of which sets the scene for the use of sputum
in fabricating potent symbols of contempt. Spitting at
someone is a profound violation.

The asymmetry – the inequality – of the one who
spits and the one who is spat upon is profound: it cuts to
the existential bedrock of the power relations between
humans. To head off talk of alpha males, pecking or-
ders and other explanatory gestures using ethological
clichés, I want to consider an instance which may surprise you, given the secular humanism proclaimed in
the previous essay.

It is captured in this line from Handel's *Messiah*:

He hid not His face from shame and spitting

– which is arresting as well as poignant. The He in
question is Jesus Christ on His way to the final ordeal.
The image of the Son of God, with sputum trickling
down his sweat-glistening, blood-stained cheek is a
shocking confrontation with the profound notion of
the Creator taking on the human condition; with the
Everywhere, Everything and All-time being robed in a
parish of flesh; with His Omnipotence voluntarily sub-
mitting to the impotence of humanity. It is not necessary to believe the myth to acknowledge its profundity

or – and this is my point – the profundity of the species that entertains it.

In this powerful myth of Christ's Passion, the strange process whereby human beings transform naturally occurring events (in this case the upwelling of saliva in their own mouths) into actively generated symbols achieves an extraordinary reach. What makes this instance even more striking is that, according to the Bible, it was foretold in the book of the prophet Isaiah seven hundred or more years before Christ is supposed to have been born. Thus is a private biological event incorporated into collective consciousness in the form of a shared myth in an act of spitting prepared seven hundred years before the soldier hurled the prophesied saliva at its target. And even if it were without historical foundation, it would be no less remarkable that we humans should incorporate such homely material – ejected sputum – into a story about the origin and purpose of the world.

The transformation of saliva into a symbol with such potency and so many ramifications illustrates what happens when we humans get our heads together. Rather less low-key, but just as extraordinary in its way, is the use I made of my own saliva the other day to glue together the strands of the cotton I was trying to thread through the top of a bauble I wanted to hang on a Christmas tree in order to celebrate in my own secular way the birth of the Child who was later spat upon *en route* to crucifixion.

NOTES ON HEAD-WINDS

No creature that has such a relationship to the secretions produced by its own head is going to be entirely straightforward. And the same applies *a fortiori* to beings that exploit the air in which they are obligatorily immersed as humans do. Humankind has appropriated the transactions necessary to ensure (among other things) an adequate intake of oxygen and a competent disposal of carbon dioxide for purposes unimaginable to any of the other beasts who, like us, also spend their lives breathing in and breathing out. I will postpone consideration of the most obvious of these purposes – speech – to pay a flying visit to something whose profound significance is rather underestimated: laughter.

'Man is the only animal who laughs and weeps; for he is the only animal that is struck with the difference between how things are and how they ought to be,' William Hazlitt said. As a philosopher would put it: *H. sapiens* uniquely has a *normative* sense. The human head is the only object in the universe that expresses amusement at other objects in the universe, focussing most often on objects that are subjects. The 'normative panting' of laughter is striking, not the least because this seemingly spontaneous, even uncontrolled, activity is highly structured and codified. We are sensitive to a multitude of carefully crafted meanings reflected in a profusion of gelastic dialects: chuckling, chortling, giggling, sniggering, braying, hooting, and so on. Different modes of laughter have different levels of *gravitas*. Giggling and sniggering, for example, is better suited to the immature than to someone like myself who is sufficiently advanced in maturity to bear unequivocal signs of rotting. Laughter can be a signature tune: there are some people whose propensity to laughter and the manner in which they laugh almost defines them in our minds; and others for whom the nervous laugh seems an inescapable accompaniment of any social occasion. Like crying, laughter may be cultivated for its own sake: we gather together to have a laugh (students do it all the time) and we pay good money to be amused, to exercise our lungs in 'normative' or 'judgemental' breathing.

There are many other minor modes of head-winding. Coughing, yawning, sneezing, hiccupping, belching, sighing, tut-tutting, harrumphing, whistling, are some. Each of these may have had an original natural or biological purpose, though the purpose of yawning is unclear. But even where they have apparent biological functions – as in the case of coughing, which prevents the lungs turning to rock as they gradually fill with insects, dust, secretions and sundry detritus – we put them to entirely different uses. We not only yawn but *employ* yawns to signal boredom or to assert our solidarity with others who are being subordinated to the same third-party empowered to inflict his views upon us at unconscionable length. More cheerfully, exhaled air may be transformed into music or song, enhanced perhaps by a wind instrument so that it may be trumpeted, bassooned, or fluted. Our lungs would be non-plussed if they knew what was happening to the stale air they were expelling.

Of all the headwinds, the most extraordinary is, of course, speech, by which in dialogue we convey meant meaning to each other through symbols manufactured for that purpose. Many things have meaning – clouds mean rain, spots mean measles, growling means hostility – but only humans mean meaning to the extent that we do. Like thermals that cause distant mountains to seem to tremble, so our thoughts, made outward and audible in puffs of air, have changed the face of the earth. Interactive headwinding is the basis of culture, of science, of history; of the sharing of experience with friends and with crowds that extend beyond our immediate neighbours to millions scattered over the surface of the earth now and in ages past.

It is arresting to think of the power of these little breezes that issue from our heads; of the transformative force of an activity that is often dismissed with the literally accurate term of 'gassing'. Most of the distances we have travelled from our natural state – measured by entire landscapes of artefacts and technologies that surround us, institutions within which and to which our lives relate, laws that direct us, preoccupations that consume us, art that delights and elevates us, explicit pasts and futures that enclose us, and the extraordinary fact that we lead our lives rather than merely live them – have been courtesy of these oral zephyrs mysteriously laden with meaning.

Speech makes present and audible that which is absent and abstract. Words give possibility a million local habitations with their million names. Chatter-borne 'thatter' – thoughts that claim or seek truth – is as influential in determining the nature of our environment as matter. Words accompany us from morning to night, from the end of infancy to the last anecdote of our dotage. When we are not speaking out loud, we are addressing ourselves in the windless speech of thought. We talk ourselves into and out of emotions – fear, hope, anticipation – into and out of plans, even into and out of plans for talk. We instruct, encourage, and guide ourselves. We discover, invent and narrate ourselves. We even speak in dreams and dream that we are speaking.

The capacity for complex speech is common to all human societies and it has played a key role in putting the *sapiens* into *Homo*. It is a relative newcomer – at the most 200,000 years old, a few seconds in the 4,000,000,000-year history of life. After an inordinate delay, the human voice joined the rustling of leaves, the scratching of crickets and the howling of wolves in the chorus of sounds on the curved surface of the earth. It is perhaps less surprising that speech came so late than that it came at all, in view of the extraordinary oro-pharyngeal micro-gymnastics necessary to articulate the simplest sentence with sufficient sharpness for its reference, its tone, and its intention to be understood. Of course, our heads are free to fashion these exquisitely sculptured head-winds hour after hour because, for much of the time, our mouths, unlike those of other beasts, are not busy grazing, catching dinner, chewing meat, sniffing each other's bottoms, or weaving nests.

At any rate, it is above all because of our ability to transform expiration into information, expired air into sometimes inspired thoughts, that we live in a distinctive realm in which is made explicit what is the case, what was the case, what will be the case, what might be the case, what ought to be the case. Speech is the mother of shared meaning, of the narrated self, of history and myth.

The human world is, as much as anything, a limitless space of multi-loculated possibility inflated by headwinds.

AIRLESS SIGNALS

Speech does not, of course, work alone. In particular, it transforms even those airless signals that play such a part in modulating our interactions with each other. The meaning of smiles, glares, and winks is greatly enriched by the sea of discourse into which they are released. Soundless smiles find their referents and significance in the echo chamber of sentences. The target of menacing glares is illuminated by hostile words.

Winks would be as empty as blinks in absence of prior definition of the winked-at that is to be subverted.

Of course signals may also be involuntary – our faces may 'betray' us as the saying goes – but they are no less profound in their occasions for that. Think of blushing, which tells the world that we are embarrassed and so makes us more embarrassed, undressing our sense of our own nakedness. Our burning cheeks turn the other's gaze into a burning glass.

The causes of blushing may be very obvious but with us humans the obvious often has deep and arcane causes. I once devoted the best part of a chapter to uncovering what I called 'the geology' of one particular blush. It lit up on the face of a man who was needlessly embarrassed at having pronounced the letter 'h' as 'haitch' with an aspirated beginning. His anxiety about the possibility of dropping an aitch had led him to the familiar over-correction – the redundant 'aitch' in 'haitch'. The crimson that spread over his face was due to the dilatation of the facial veins; but this physiological reaction had profound causes.

Not only did the blush require that there should be such a thing as speech but also: that speech should be written down; that inscription should be decomposed into letters; that letters should have names; and that the names of the letters should have a correct or an incorrect pronunciation; and that pronunciation should be a 'shibboleth' locating the speaker in a particular social group. By looking at the blush in this way, it is possible – as is so often the case – to use a trivium of everyday life as a glass bottomed boat through which to fathom the depths of the distinctly human.

BRIEF DIGRESSIONS

It might seem appropriate to stop here and return to the home key and my main theme: automated thanks and other sundry performatives, what they tell us about our human nature, and the notion of 'exographic storage'. I cannot, however, resist hovering a little more over our consciousness if only to highlight the gulf between ourselves and even our nearest primate kin, and the scale of the challenge facing anyone who wants to characterise the gap and explain how it opened up.

Let's begin with space. A review of the spaces into which my consciousness has been deployed would encompass: the idea of the North; homes remembered from various modes of abroad; workplaces and playplaces; a garden defined by hedges, a kitchen with a half-open door, and a locked filing cabinet; and a muddle of 'vicinities' and 'next tos' and 'nearbys' tethered to and shaped by the presence of persons, facilities and goals, that lie beyond the competence of the geometer to capture. Closeness and distance, 'over here' and 'over there', have distinctly non-Euclidean boundaries and surfaces, defined by limits midway between the literal edges of tables and pavements and metaphorical

ones like the verge of a lost temper or of a tempta-
tion succumbed to. Such are the spaces of our lives,
Chinese-boxed one into another, ranging in scale from
national boundaries patrolled by border guards, to city
limits marked by printed welcomes, rooms curtained
against the gaze of strangers and private places where
access is regulated by zips and buttons. These are the
spaces we unpack in lives that occupy a very narrow
band of scales between the physical limits of the very
small (the effective diameter of a proton of around 10^{-15}
centimetres) and the very large (the visible universe
10^{19} times the radius of the planet, the earth, that contains all our wanderings).

Among the smallest of such spaces – a cupful of
warmth in Galaxy-wide cold – your essayist, looking
to add a pinch of self to season this exploration of
human consciousness, remembers the pockets of his
short trousers where a lozenge had fastened itself to a
farthing. The wren had taken off from the coin – that
had fallen below the threshold for legal tender as he
had entered adolescence – when a real wren in a garden, fifty years later, magnifying the presence of its few
grams through twigs it made to twitch, had reminded
him of the bird (*verso* to the *recto* head of a sovereign
much younger then than now).

Thus the exquisite ways that my past, the ordinary
past of an instance of humanity, insists in the present.
Time for another pinch of self. I am running on a treadmill. To while away the time until the target distance of

300 metres is achieved, I locate myself on the 22 tram in Prague, stand up as my stop approaches, alight, examine the ornate shop label next to the tram stop, look right and left and right again (unnerved by wrong-side traffic), ascend Ruska street, pause at the carved violinist at number 15, look to the left at the balconied apartments in Estovska, recite the other intersecting roads, reach number 60, fumble for the key and find that I have completed my prescribed distance.

Thus the internal cognitive stitching of an ordinary 21st-century human consciousness, that looks forward to Christmas (when a partridge would be repeatedly drawn to a pear tree by the same force of alliteration as made lords leap in unison), exercises his mind over whether his namesake's 40-part motet was written to celebrate the 40th birthday of a sovereign who had died over 350 years before he had been born, and worries whether he has remembered to transfer his senior rail pass to the jacket he is wearing as he enters a station to buy a rail ticket.

Such pinches of self prompt thoughts about the relationship between our biographies and their passing moments; between the scaffolding of the CV and the in-between spaces in which it was enacted or suffered, the story on the canvas and the lived pixels; the dialectic between the nested structures and the moments that made sense of them.

All of this is easily lost from view. And, by an irony that is built into our cognitive structures, the

very means by which our sense of the profundity of
the human is numbed − jokes, clichés, gassing (*vide
supra*), a knowingness passing itself off as knowledge
that summarises a town, India, history, and humanity
in a few lazy words − are further folds in our profundity. We may be appalled by the recent use of the First
World War in an advert to promote mince pies (don't
ask) but we should also be astounded at the ingenuity
with which we cancel the profundity of our awareness
of that gigantic catastrophe.

At any rate, such astonishment is too often kept
severely in check by the habitual gaze, the habitual feel-
ings, the habitual thoughts that are over-accustomed to
themselves and their objects. They apply to the mani-
fest world a thick and tenacious patina that becomes
evident when we want to see the light folded away in
what Martin Heidegger called 'everydayness' and we
try to think to the heart of our daily actuality. It is only
because we are so strange that we are able to find ourselves and our lives ordinary.

In the spirit of showing my − your, our − complexity instead of going on abstractly about it, I could list
some of the 'last times' before the final last time of my
last breath. The last time: I used my index finger as
a shoehorn and remembered being chided for breaking down the backs of my shoes; snapped my fingers
to look cool; explicitly had a double-take or doubted
the validity of an argument; winced at the pleonasm
'new innovation'; refused the offer of beetroot (a life-

long aversion); made custard the butt of a joke; crossed an earlier path in my crisscrossing the surface of the earth; was sceptical of an overheard comment about 'bank rate rise'; enjoyed a conclusive bowel action; ignored the exhortation to be alert for signs of terrorist activity; used a newspaper to mop up spilt water; was told to buck up my ideas or buckled a buckle; consciously lolled or coasted; proposed a toast; imagined a future event or state of myself, of another, or of a part of the world; took a deep breath and pronounced it a 'lungful'; used the definite article.

Thus a sample of the humanity that 'secular humanism' charges itself with defending.

EXOGRAPHIC STORAGE AND AUTO-CUEING

And so we return to the place where we digressed some while back; namely, my being thanked by a paper bag and the concept of 'exographic storage'. The term was coined by Merlin Donald, a Canadian psychologist, cognitive neuroscientist, and profound thinker in the field of philosophical anthropology. So, thanks to the courtesy of paper bags, I have an opportunity to introduce this great thinker to some people who (like me only a few years ago) had not heard of him.

Donald has thought long and hard about the roots of the distinctively human consciousness. He is exercised by the vastness of the cognitive gap between human beings and their nearest primate kin, the chimpanzees. It is a gap whose scale that many thinkers, particularly evolutionary psychologists, have, deliberately or inadvertently, resisted acknowledging. The reason for their odd behaviour is the groundless fear that to do so, and to admit the uniqueness of humanity, would put Darwinian Theory in question and threaten a regression to pre-Darwinian, possibly religious, accounts of our nature and origin. Professor Donald, and your essayist, disagree. Admitting to the vast cognitive gulf between human persons and non-human primates does not require us to believe that the human *organism* was created by non-Darwinian processes. It does however mean that we have some explaining to do; to give some account of how the organism *H. sapiens* got to be so different; and that requires examining in what fundamental respects humans are different from other primates. This is what Donald has attempted in a series of contributions to the debate on the evolution of human consciousness.

He has traced its fascinating journey to the present where, for example, gratitude may be expressed by a paper bag. Thanks, welcomes, warnings, apologies and so in the absence of anyone doing the thanking, welcoming, warning, and apologising, are striking illustrations of our ability to deposit ourselves outside of ourselves on to insentient surfaces. This is what Donald calls 'exographic storage'. Inscription – writing on bark, paper, or electronic media – is the most obvious manifestation of this, though it is implicitly or explicitly present throughout the landscape of artefacts in which we pass our lives. We take it rather too much for granted. So we must go a long way back and see what writing, and indeed speech, presuppose; what has already to be in place for them to be possible.

Donald identifies three major cognitive transformations by which the human mind emerged over millions of years, starting out from a complex of skills presumably resembling those we see in chimpanzees. (Summarised in an excellent paper *Précis of the Origin of the Modern Mind: Three Stages in the Evolution of Culture and Cognition.*) They underpin the passage from the non-symbolic cognitions of animals to the fully symbolic representations that are wall-to-wall in everyday human life.

The first transformation was the acquisition by early hominids of the ability to use the body as a representational device. These mimetic skills – evident in gestures and mime – based on an abstract model of the body, allowed actions to be stopped, replayed, and edited under conscious control. Donald links this mimetic ability with self-teaching and the refinement of action by deliberate repetition. It underlies our unique agency which has enabled us 'to break the stranglehold of the environment'. Consciously refined motor activity, based on the mimetic capacity of a creature distanced to some extent from its own body, is the basis not only of the meant meanings conveyed by gestures but also of the first customs that form the background social theatre that supports and structures group behaviour in modern humans.

A crucial capacity underpinning mimetic skills is 'auto-cueing'. This is the ability to access the contents of your memories of particular experiences independently of environmental prompts, enabling actions to be initiated not only on the basis of external triggers but also self-generated cues. Man is the only creature who racks his brains. Remember your essayist requisitioning the journey from the 22 tram to number 60 Ruska in a capital city hundreds of miles distance from his brain to while away the time on the treadmill. (And, come to that, he is always devising plots to outwit his own forgetfulness, thinking up new ways of ambushing himself with reminders.) The capacity voluntarily to access and retrieve experiences and outputs is a necessary condition of many other cognitive and motor skills, including the already referred to self-teaching with a view to developing, correcting, and modifying complex patterns of behaviour.

The revolution in nonverbal motor skills was, Donald convincingly argues, a necessary bridge to the next cognitive transformation: lexical invention – the ability to create an expanding vocabulary. He regards language as even more of a newcomer than do other writers, emerging perhaps 50,000 years ago. At any rate, it is a *parvenu* compared with the capacity for mimesis just discussed which may be up to 1.5 million years old. The emergence of this new, linguistic, mode of representation, with a vocabulary and a grammar, was dependent on an already established capacity to generate rehearsable and retrievable vocal acts. The point is that, according to Donald, language arose in humans only because they were already cognitively remote from their primate predecessors. This will explain the disappointing results of attempts to get chimps to speak: they don't have the cognitive infrastructure. In short, they don't get it. At the risk of sounding chimpist, it appears that chimps are chumps.

Donald's account of the emergence and evolution of language is (as it should be) extremely complex and there is no space to treat it adequately here. And so I hasten on to the third transition, which is most directly relevant to my being thanked by a paper bag. Donald calls this 'the externalisation of memory'. It is driven primarily by technological rather than biological developments. Amongst its many extraordinary effects has been the emergence of a shared representational culture no longer dependent on or constrained by individual memory. The consequences of externalising what is internal 'deepens the internal and this is turn extends the external'. The gap between ourselves and our nearest primate kin widens.

Which brings us to the now almost infinitely varied modes of *inscription* or (to repeat Donald's term), 'exographic storage' which is a mere few thousand years old. The consequences have been dramatic. The most immediate and most obvious include: the expansion and pooling of the available past (and its mirror, the anticipated future); the accumulation of knowledge; the development of theories based on information laid out for inspection, contemplation, and interrogation; and the limitless amplification of technology-based capabilities.

Most relevant to our present concerns, however, is the establishment of a collective public realm. The relationship between the individual mind and the community of minds created out of what I have described elsewhere as 'a trillion cognitive handshakes' becomes ever more elaborate. We have been able to put our heads together to create a community of minds whose fruits are all around, and indeed within, us. This community of minds, or our participation in it, is not located in our stand alone brains and their electrochemical processes, because we have transcended our individual brains.

And this has a transformative effect on our relationship to each other, most strikingly evident in the way we communicate, and who is communicating with whom. The who and the whom may be a general, an abstractly conceived audience, defined by certain situations and the propensities of putative addressees. Which brings me back finally to the gratitude of paper bags.

Those millions of thanks – standardised representations of symbolic actions disconnected from any bodies, from any speaking mouth, even (since they are machine-stamped) from a writing hand – addressed by no-one in particular to no-one in particular, are a paradigm instance of our exographic mode of being. The long journey of cognitive evolution leading from our primate predecessors is illuminated by this humble example.

We are insufficiently astonished by our heads and the things we have achieved by putting our heads together. It is fashionable at present to be disgusted by, scornful of, dismissive of, cynical about, humanity. Misanthropy of the kind propagated by the philosopher John Gray, who in *Straw Dogs* (he of the 'slime mould') speaks of humanity as *Homo rapiens*, is in the ascendant. In response to this badmouthing, I would point out that, by putting our heads together, we have been able to achieve what Munchausen only boasted of: we have lifted ourselves above the organic material of which we ourselves are made. Our lives are wall-to-wall with events that are remote from anything prescribed by our organic being, even when they are rooted in biological need. Humankind has increasingly made the world its own thing by transforming and understanding that world. We should be therefore astonished at, rather than contemptuous of, the 'unreasonable effectiveness' of our collective consciousness in making effective, ordinary, daily sense of the world.

'Out of the crooked timber of humanity, no straight thing was ever made,' the German philosopher

Immanuel Kant famously said. Given the material out of which we are made and self-made, it is amazing just how straight we are at times and just how much of the world around us we seem to have got straight. Collectively, we have created a space of possibility – the boundless-in-all-directions human world – unknown to the natural world. It is limitless space of knowledge that includes the knowledge that it is located in a space that is as near to being infinite as makes no difference.

And so it is my turn to give thanks – to Professor Donald. Whether or not you accept his account of the steps by which we came to be so different, his theories have highlighted the extraordinary nature of human beings and their capacity to externalise their own consciousness.

And thanks, too, to the paper bag for a printed gratitude reminding me how even the seemingly shallowest manifestations of our shared consciousness have profound roots.

3

– How on Earth Can We Be Free? –

> All theory is against the freedom of the will; all experience is for it.
> – Dr Johnson, quoted in Boswell's *Life*

I am in my late sixties, but I still find I am arguing against my fifteen-year-old self, though that self is more likely to be represented by certain contemporary writers than by Raymond Tallis. This is never truer than when I am thinking about freedom of the will. The thought that everything I did was determined by forces outside of me, so that I was not in any worthwhile sense an independent agent, caused me considerable anguish in my early teens. It seemed to make any attempt to shape my life and the future that then lay ahead of me futile. There were also homelier reasons: I might not, for example, be able to take credit for the successes I had had in my examinations or for the effort that made them possible – a much-needed source of self-esteem.

Questions of free will and determinism remain live issues in philosophy. And so they should. Our freedom is central to our human dignity. Acceptance of personal responsibility is a *sine qua non* of a flourishing secular society. While there have been distinguished philosophers in the Western tradition such as Lucretius, Thomas Hobbes and Spinoza, denying that we have free will, historically the main assault on the idea of humans as free agents has come from religion. An omnipotent God has, for some, implied an 'omnimpotent' (*sic*) humanity, though such claims have paradoxically been accompanied by exhortations to choose the good life with divine threats of judgement and punishment for those who don't.

More recently, however, the case against our freedom has been founded less on the implacable Will of God who moves in a mysterious way than on the largely invisible operation of the unbreakable Laws of Nature. Denial of our free will is potentially the most damaging of the consequences of the philosophical naturalism according to which we are variously construed as material objects or organisms, a view wrongly embraced by many humanists as the only alternative to a supernatural understanding of humanity.

Naturalistic fatalism has recently been boosted by apparent support from the biological sciences, notably neuroscience. The general idea is that our actions and reactions are the products of evolved brains that themselves have been shaped by material influences of which we are incompletely aware and over which we have no ultimate control. The prestige of neuroscience has fostered the faith that its findings are relevant to the essentially metaphysical question of whether or not humans can truly be authors of their actions. The dissemination of this belief beyond academe – so that 'your brain made you do it' has become a widely received idea – makes critical examination urgent.

Before launching into a defence of free will, it is important to clarify what is on trial. Robert Kane's definition (in *The Significance of Free Will*) – 'the power of agents to be the ultimate creators (or originators) and sustainers of their own ends and purposes' – is a good start. Freedom of the will implies that we can truly say of at least some of our behaviour 'the buck starts with me'; that our actions have deflected the course of events; that they express something within us that we can truly own; and that what we have done is one of several possibilities genuinely open to us such that we could have done or chosen otherwise.

It is important to underline what belief in free will does *not* commit us to. It does not require us to believe that *everything* an agent does is free, that every part of a free action is explicitly done and freely executed, or that the agent is free to do anything. This – the limitation and dependency of our freedom – is something to which I will return.

DETERMINISM

The traditional case against free will must be one of the most familiar in philosophy and is easily stated. It goes as follows: Actions are physical events. Every physical event has a prior physical cause which in turn has a prior cause. The causal chain that led up to 'my' actions – which in theory could be traced back to the Big Bang – ultimately originates in events over which I have no control. Everything I (seemingly) do is thus the remote effect of happenings which I have not initiated. My actions are no more mine, in the sense of originating with me, than are their causal ancestors, most of which will have taken place before I was born. We could make the same point slightly differently. Actions (including their motivations) are part of the boundless causal nexus of the material universe. There is nothing outside this causal nexus. The world, as the philosophers say, is causally closed.

We could advance a complementary argument grounded in the laws of nature. The universe and everything in it (including ourselves) evolve according to absolutely general laws which by definition are unbreakable. The combination of initial conditions and laws will fix the overall state of the universe at any given time. There are no exceptions, not even for the material object that is the human body or brain, assumed to be identical with the human person. Finally, my very existence – the necessary condition of my performing any actions at all – was not chosen by myself nor did I choose the general properties, and particular circumstances, of the body underpinning my existence.

We seem, in sum, to be soluble fish in a sea of law-governed causation. How, therefore, could there be any possibility that we could deflect the order of things, that we could initiate or be the *origin* of events that we could count as our own?

I want to set aside arguments based on recent developments in physics – at the risk of seeming ungrateful for small mercies. Some defenders of free will have seized on the replacement of causation by probability at the subatomic level investigated by quantum mechanics, according to which there is no linear dictation of particular events as a consequence of particular causes. This is unhelpful. We do not live, and actions are not planned, or executed, at the subatomic level. No agent known to me is subatomic and such entities are not free. Besides, this would be of little help since the individual random quantum events conform to a set of fixed probabilities expressed in frequencies that are predefined to many more decimal points than are perceptible in everyday life. They don't provide any more elbow room than the most rigid causal connectedness.

The other argument from physics is even weaker. The great French scientist Laplace asserted that, given a complete statement of initial conditions and a comprehensive set of laws, we could predict what will happen in any part of the universe whether it was a star or a human being. It has recently been noted that Laplacean prediction founders on the fact that minute changes in initial conditions can quickly result in vast differences in outcome. Complex systems are entirely unpredictable. This does not, however, prove that the physical world is not deterministic, only that its future is difficult to determine. If unpredictability were sufficient for freedom, then weather systems (notoriously chaotic) would be some of the freest entities on earth. Does anyone imagine that Hurricane Katrina was responsible for the damage it wreaked in New Orleans?

What free will requires is not randomness or unpredictability in the material world but *control* of it. Unpredictability and chaos are hardly the conditions of freedom. What's more, loosely textured laws would not widen the space for agency, given that we need nature to be utterly reliable if our actions are to have their intended consequences.

So there is no escape from determinism coming from this direction. The case against free will seems unanswerable. And it will remain so as long as we accept the implicit premises of the argument; namely that the world within which we act as agents is the world as described by natural science: a causally closed world governed by physical laws. A defence of the possibility of freedom must challenge those assumptions. Before we do so, we need to confront a more specific endeavour, tailored to our supposed nature as living brains, to discredit our claims to be free.

NEURODETERMINISM

At the heart of the claim that neuroscience has something to say on the question of free will is the increasingly widely accepted assumption that minds, persons, selves, are brains. Brains are physical objects and are therefore subject to the laws of nature. There is a particular inflection of this idea: our brains are evolved organs designed (as are all organs) by natural selection to maximize the replicative ability of the genes whose tool they are. We are largely unaware of this. For many writers this means that we are at the behest of a biological script at odds with the humanist story we tell ourselves about ourselves as conscious agents.

The difference between matter and living matter is regarded as purely superficial. This is captured in a well-known passage from the philosopher Daniel Dennett in *Consciousness Explained*:

There is only one sort of stuff, namely *matter* – the physical stuff of physics, chemistry and physiology – and the mind is somehow nothing but a physical phenomenon. In short, the mind is the brain . . . We can (in principle!) account for every mental phenomenon using the same physical principles, laws and raw materials that suffice to explain radioactivity, continental drift, photosynthesis, reproduction, nutrition and growth.

If people are their brains (in fact they are not, as I have argued in *Aping Mankind: Neuromania,*

Darwinitis and the Misrepresentation of Humanity), they are identified with a piece of matter and this, like all other pieces of matter, is subject to, and cannot escape from, the laws of material nature. Everything that happens in our brains is the product of material events that impinge on them and the events that result from brain activity – notably our actions – are wired into the endless causal net, extending from the Big Bang to the Big Crunch. Minds and persons are embedded in the physical world. Our destiny, like that of pebbles and waterfalls, is to be pre-destined.

This specifically neuroscientific case against free will is expressed with exemplary clarity by the eminent neuroscientist Colin Blakemore (in *The Mind Machine*):

The human brain is a machine which alone accounts for all our actions, our most private thoughts, our beliefs . . . It makes no sense (in scientific terms) to try to distinguish sharply between acts that result from conscious attention and those that result from our reflexes or are caused by disease or damage to the brain.

If we are identical with our brains, or certain neural discharges in them, we must be just as unfree when we are writing a textbook about the management of seizures, or (as Blakemore has done) giving Reith lectures on the brain, as when we ourselves are in the grip of a seizure: it 'makes no sense in *neuro*scientific terms' to distinguish between these things.

Many philosophers have pitched in on the side of the neuro-determinist scientists. This is philosopher Mark Balaguer (*Free Will as an Open Scientific Problem*):

The metaphysically interesting issue in the problem of free will and determinism boils down to a straightforward (and wide open) empirical question about the causal histories of certain neural events.

Balaguer – as have many others – has invoked data from neurosciences that seem to eat into our freedom. He notes that: conscious awareness of actions and processes lags behind the processes themselves; people are frequently mistaken about why they perform certain actions; our actions are often significantly influenced by situational factors whose importance we have not noticed; and conscious and seemingly free choices can be influenced by brain stimulation.

Many other writers have adduced the evidence from neurophysiology and cognitive psychology that seems to uncover the unconscious influences on what we notice and how we behave. Thousands of 'priming' experiments have demonstrated that what we recall or pay particular attention to may be manipulated by exposing us to adjacent or associated stimuli that we are not aware of: we have registered them without registering that we register them. A much cited experiment seemed to show that our willingness to give to beggars, far from being a pure expression of our ethical or political principles, may be increased (without our being aware of it) if the beggar locates close to a bakery emitting the scent of baked bread that gives us a sense of well-being. So-called 'nominal determinism' suggests that even a crucial, large decision such as choice of profession is in part determined by your first name: so people called Dennis are more likely to elect to become dentists. And there are many researchers who have established to their own satisfaction that even in our most creative moments − when we seem to be expressing the highest levels of freedom − that it is our unconscious that is in charge.

Many of these studies are poorly designed and their significance has been overestimated; but it has not stopped writers concluding as does psychologist Daniel Wegner (in *The Illusion of the Conscious Will*) that: 'the only connexion between willing and acting is that both come from the same unconscious source'. Or as Sam Harris (*Free Will*), a hard-line atheist committed to scientism, put it:

Free will is an illusion . . . Thoughts and intentions emerge from background causes of which [we] are unaware and over which we exert no conscious control.

The most striking apparent support for the neuro-determinists has come from hugely influential experimental studies of what happens in the brain during seemingly voluntary action. These studies are worth examining because they highlight (by default) what is missing in much of the debate on determinism; namely an analysis of the nature of action.

Let us first look at a famous set of experiments, carried out by the neurophysiologist Benjamin Libet in the 1980s ('Unconscious Cerebral Initiative and the Role of Conscious Will in Involuntary Action') and repeated and refined many times since then. They have seemed to some to show that our brain makes decisions to act before our conscious mind is aware of them, so they are not really *our* decisions at all. So what did Libet do and what did he find?

In a typical experiment, Libet's subjects are instructed to make a simple movement – such as to bend their wrist or the fingers of a hand – in their own time. Using an electroencephalogram, the experimenter records a particular activity in the brain that indicates a readiness to move. This so-called 'readiness potential' (RP) is seen in the part of the cerebral cortex most closely associated with voluntary movement. The RP occurs about half a second before activity in the relevant muscles of the arm or hand, as recorded by an electromyogram, because it takes time for the neural activity in the cortex to translate into events in the relevant muscles.

Nothing worrying there. But Libet made another observation that seemed to raise serious questions. He asked his subjects to recall the position occupied by a spot revolving round a clock face in order to determine the time when they were first aware of their urge or intention to make a movement. To his surprise, he found that the RP occurred a consistent third of a second *before* the time at which the subjects reported being aware of a decision to move. Libet concluded from this that the *brain* 'decided' to initiate, or at least to prepare to initiate, the act before there was any reportable subjective awareness of a decision having been made. Put more simply, the cerebral causes of our actions seem to occur *before* our conscious awareness of deciding to perform them.

These findings are open to a range of interpretations, as we shall see, but they cannot be dismissed as mere artefacts of the method of recording, though as has been shown recently, we infer rather than directly perceive the moment we decide to act. Nor can the gap between the electrical signal of the initiation of action, the RP, and the awareness of the intention to perform the action be explained away as simply being the interval between forming an intention and being sufficiently reflectively aware of the intention to allocate it to a particular time. That this is so has been demonstrated rather dramatically by more recent work, this time using a more powerful method of imaging activity in the waking brain – functional magnetic resonance imaging.

In 2008, John Dylan-Haynes and his team carried out studies ('Unconscious determinants of free decisions in the human brain') in which subjects elected to press a button with their left or right hand at a moment of their own choosing. At the same time, a succession of letters was displayed on a screen and subjects were required to note the letter being displayed at the time they felt that they were making a decision to press the button. The letter was a time marker, rather like the clock in Libet's experiment. Two regions that lit up in the brain predicted the subject's choice of left or right button. Remarkably, the regions in question (in the part of the cerebral cortex associated with voluntary movement) lit up *a full five seconds* before the individual was aware of having made a choice so the scientists could tell which button was going to be pressed. Moreover, there were other areas in the frontal cortex, traditionally ascribed executive powers that were active no less than *seven* seconds before awareness of the decision. If the delay in the response of the scanner detecting the activity was accounted for, the interval increased to *ten* seconds. Such a delay could not be due to the subject mistiming the intention to move – a possible explanation for Libet's original findings, since it is somewhat tricky to time one's own decisions. The authors concluded that there is a network of high-level control areas 'that begins to prepare an upcoming decision long before it enters awareness'.

It looks like we don't know what we are doing until we have found that we have done it.

THE STORY SO FAR

The case for free will is looking pretty ropy. There are *a priori* arguments for thinking that we are not the authors of our actions; that what we claim as 'our' actions or which are ascribed to us as the manifestation of our agency, are just events that pass through us, expressing laws over which we have no control, or parts of a causal chain that began before we began and will end (if at all) long after we have ended. These *a priori* arguments seem to be supported by observations that show that our brains are in charge. We are the playthings of an organ whose behaviour is determined by an evolutionary script over which we have no more sovereignty than we have over our kidneys.

Before we leap to the defence of free will, it is perhaps timely to reflect on the oddness of having to defend something no-one really doubts. An assumption of the reality of our agency – such that we may be justly held responsible by ourselves and others for our actions – permeates every aspect of daily life. Would anyone deny the difference between being hit by a ball on the head and positioning ourselves to catch it? We believe there is a fundamental difference between falling down the stairs, walking down them as the first part of a journey to another town for a meeting, and creeping down the stairs in such a way as not to wake the baby. We routinely contrast those events for which we seem to be directly responsible with those for which we can hardly be held responsible. And, finally, we identify circumstances under which we seem to be less free than others – as when, for example, we are asleep or in a coma. None of these distinctions would make any kind of sense if there were no fundamental difference between events that merely happen to us and things that we *initiate*.

In reality, few people who deny our freedom do so sincerely. Consider, for example, this revealing quote from Ivan Pavlov:

Our belief in our freedom of the will will fade and, moreover, our mastery over ourselves will gain much specificity from a greater and greater understanding of the physiological mechanisms of our brain activity.
– *Notes*, 1926

It seems that once, courtesy of science, we realise we are not free we shall become more free in virtue of gaining more control of ourselves! And I presume that it had not escaped Sam Harris' attention that his book was published by the Free Press – dedicated to freedom of speech, which rather presupposes more fundamental freedoms.

It is time to mount our defence.

AGAINST NEURODETERMINISM

Let me start with a relatively soft target: neurodeterminism. Consider the claims from psychology and other neuroscience disciplines that we are less free than we think we are – on the grounds that we are sometimes susceptible to unconscious influences or we find we have done things without thinking about them or we are sometimes more likely to follow emotions rather than reasons. These do not demonstrate that there is no such thing as freedom. If action A is *less* free than action B, though both seem to the actor to be genuinely voluntary, this does not prove that both, or all, actions are unfree. 'More free' and 'less free' still presuppose freedom. The experiments carried out by Libet and by Dylan-Haynes and his team, however, require more detailed critical examination. I will argue that they have nothing to say about the exercise of free will in the real world, for two principal reasons.

Firstly, the actions that the experimenters required of their subjects were utterly trivial. The choice between left and right hand was lacking in any significance. Nothing was at stake and nothing of material importance to the subject was engaged. Indeed, the 'action' hardly counted as an action at all: a mere movement such as pressing a button or moving the wrist. The button was not attached to anything that mattered to the subject and the movement was not even a signal such as pointing or thumbs up.

Secondly (and of much greater significance as we shall see), these trivial actions were in fact only *fragments* of actions that belonged to something much bigger – something called 'taking part in a laboratory experiment' – most of which was beyond the scope of the experiment and the laboratory. This large-scale action, to which the finger movements owed any sense and purpose they had, began at least as far back as getting up in the morning to visit the laboratory (after, perhaps, setting the alarm to make sure one was not late); involved consenting to take part in a procedure whose nature, purpose and safety was fully understood; and required (among many other things) listening to and understanding and agreeing to the instructions that were received – and *then* deciding to flex the wrist. In other words, the immediate prior intention, the psychological event timed in the lab, was not the whole, or even a significant part of the story of the action, only a tiny part of it. It was preceded by many relevant events that were minutes, hours, perhaps days, before the action.

The real story was not just the flexing of the wrist but one of a sustained and complex resolve being maintained over a very long time. This included many large items of behaviour – cancelling or declining other commitments so as to be free to honour the appointment in the laboratory, getting on and off buses, looking for the laboratory and perhaps getting cross with the poor signage, and so on – that have many thousands, perhaps hundreds of thousands, of motor components all orchestrated and subordinated to achieving a rather complex goal. None of this was, or needed to be, in play in the very brief interval between the decision to move the finger and actually moving it. But the latter made sense only with respect to an extensive suite of nested frames of references all in place well before the recorded brain activity and indeed before the experiment began.

Once this is appreciated, then the time relationship between the last step – moving the hand and the brain activity such as the Readiness Potential seen in the lab, becomes insignificant. The decision to participate in the research, which alone gave the wrist flexion its meaning, began not milliseconds, seconds, or minutes, but hours before the wrist was flexed. It may have been weeks before, when the person decided to become a subject in the experiment. The flexing of the wrist is just the last component of this action called 'taking part in an experiment' which could itself be part of a greater intentional whole, such as 'wanting to help those clever scientists understand the brain as it might one day help doctors to treat my child's brain injury more effectively'.

It now seems less disturbing (or less exciting, according to your taste) that the RP preceded the intention to make a movement by a mere 300 to 450 milliseconds, or that the brain activity seen on the scan in Dylan-Hayes' experiment was up to ten seconds in advance of the intention. Its apparent importance is owing to a simplified – and grossly distorted – notion of a free action: seeing it as the specific effect of a specific cause, namely a particular intention. In fact, the intention to flex the wrist belongs to a much wider *field* of intention which has temporal depth and wide existential salience and is connected with great swathes of the acting individual's self-world (including her knowledge, motives, principles, etc.). Our intentions are interconnected with each other as are our decisions and our plans. They are not linear pushes like local causes but part of a landscape, a fabric, of embraced significance – of our sense of who and what we are and where we are in our lives. For this reason, most actions do not have to be propelled into existence by specific intentions; for the most part they unfold without explicit decisions – except broad brush ones – at every node. When I am walking to the pub to meet you, there isn't a separate decision corresponding to every one of the hundreds of steps I take to get there. The intentions of our actions are not localised quasi-causes sited immediately before the actions.

Behind this objection to the over interpretation of the Libet and Dylan-Haynes experiments is something much bigger. Making this visible will be at the heart of our strategy to deal with the harder challenge: determinism neat.

AGAINST DETERMINISM:
LOOKING AT REAL ACTIONS

Let us not forget this: When 'I raise my arm', my arm goes up. And the problem arises: what is left over if I subtract the fact that my arm goes up from the fact that I raise my arm?

This was how the philosopher Ludwig Wittgenstein once characterized the puzzle of the elusive difference between a physical event (my arm goes up) that merely happens and an action that is performed (I raise my arm). If we are going to understand how genuinely free actions are possible, then we need to look at this difference carefully. But it will not be sufficient to investigate something as simple as raising one's hand, in isolation from the flow of the behaviour we usually take to be voluntary. Indeed, that would be a mistake. If we simplify actions in this way, we shall certainly lose what it is that makes them freely performed. Libet's experiment inadvertently illustrates how the (neuro) determinist case against freedom is rooted in a very impoverished, indeed distorted, conception of what constitutes an action in everyday life.

If you want to make voluntary actions seem involuntary the first thing you have to do is to strip away their context – the person from whom they originate, the soil from which they grow, the nexus of meanings that is the world to which they are addressed – and then effectively break them down into their physical elements. This gets you well on the way to eliminating the difference between a twitch and a deliberate action; or between, say, my *in*voluntarily taking part in the experiment, having been carried to the lab in a coma and woken up simply to move my wrist, and my participating in it because I want to help those clever scientists.

It is possible to take denaturing of actions even further. I could, for example, decompose the process of writing this essay into physiological events such as the formation and rupture of cross-bridges in the fibres of my hand muscles when they contract. Now it is perfectly obvious that I could not *do* the physiology of my movements: I would not know how to make or unmake a muscle cross-bridge if I tried. Does it follow from this that I am not writing this essay freely or that I am not really intending to write it or that it has no relation to my intentions during the days when I first started planning it? No; all that this demonstrates is that atoms of actions shorn of the frame of reference that give them meaning, cannot be separately intended, and it is misguided to look for the freedom of my free act at that level. Real actions are not made of atomic movements denuded of context. They are indissoluble wholes, orchestrated by higher order intentions that issue not from bodies but from persons. This is where our attention should be directed when we are looking for free will.

Ordinary actions incorporate vast numbers of

physical events arranged hierarchically with subordinate elements serving super-ordinate or overarching purposes. These events are *requisitioned* as the means to bring about certain intermediate ends, themselves means to further ends, often involving tools and machines that facilitate or deputize for other intermediate steps. Seen in this light, it is evident that an action is an event that would not have taken place unless it had a purpose explicitly entertained by an agent.

Consider a commonplace example such as a workout in a gym. Travelling to the destination (walking, driving, walking), changing into appropriate kit, and engaging with treadmills and other devices (a privilege for which I have paid a subscription in advance) – all these intrinsically complex steps are linked together into an action that itself is only part of a programme of activity that has the somewhat abstract aim of postponing the time when I might fall ill. I am running away not from a predator but from a possibility of illness brought to my attention by a meta-analysis of studies on dementia and exercise. Such a sequence of physical events (including those that are involved in taking out a subscription, for example, making sure that one's credit card is up to date) would not have been assembled, and arranged in a certain order, without a sustained and sustaining intention, a consciously envisaged goal, that makes them intelligible – most importantly to me. We could put this another way by saying that the chances of the succession of events comprising an action such as going to the gym occurring spontaneously as an expression of unguided laws of nature would be negligible. By contrast, the even more numerous components of a physical process such as an avalanche progressing down a mountain consists of causally interacting events that require no intelligibility, no goal for them to have happened and happened in concert.

The bespoke *sequence* of events could not be generated by the untutored *general* machinery of the laws of nature. It is tailored by an explicit, personal goal to which it is directed, such as fulfilling my target of going to the gym three times a week as recommended by the meta-analysis I have read. Which is not to say that the avalanche, too, does not have a complex backstory. The events that led up to it go back a long way; perhaps to the Big Bang if we accept that we can trace all that happens to an initial universe-creating event. But it is an entirely different kind of backstory from that which accounts for my visit to the gym. Such human behaviour, as Merlin Donald points out (in *Précis of the Origin of the Modern Mind: Three Stages in the Evolution of Culture and Cognition*) is subject to 'background planning, metacognitive oversight, and social communication'. In the case of actions, physical events are being *used* rather than merely being allowed to happen.

There are yet other characteristics of (perfectly ordinary) actions which undeniably distinguish them from other sequences of events in the material world. These differences are so profound that they justify our revisiting the assumption that 'I raise my arm' is basically a physical event identical to 'my arm goes up'.

The key assumption on which determinism rests is that actions are physical events and that therefore, like other physical events, they must be the expression of unbreakable causal laws that dictate the passage from one state of the world to the next. Our bodies – indeed our lives – are simply strands in a nexus of material events whose origin lies in the distant past. We cannot act voluntarily, it is argued, because this would seem to require that we magically prise open a causally closed world.

The assumptions appear incontrovertible only if we think of 'the human world', the theatre in which we act, as being an ordinary part of the universe as it is represented in objective physical science. The latter universe is a system of mere magnitudes – forces and energies and the like – empty of consciousness and drained of meaning. If this truly were the whole story of the human world, the very *notions* of 'cause' and of 'laws' could not arise. It is not possible to think of a cause of the *concept* of a cause or imagine a (physical) law that brought about the *idea* of a law. And of course there *are* such notions. From which it follows that this is *not* the whole story.

This may seem a rather small point to carry a large

conclusion but it is connected with another that may seem more telling. If the human world were part of the causally closed universe not only would it have no place for the notion of causes, it would not be able to accommodate the very idea of causes that are *used*. It is, however, an indisputable fact that at every moment of our lives, we pick out possible causes and indeed use them – as levers, handles, keys, and the like, to bring about envisaged effects or consequences. In sum, we are not merely subject to the laws of nature but we identify those laws – in the form of crude correlations in the case of pre-scientific humankind and more sophisticated general principles subsequently – and *exploit* them. In this respect we are utterly different from other material objects which are no more aware of the laws that govern the changes that occur in them than I am aware of the potassium ensuring that my nerve fibres are able to function.

No-one, surely, can deny that we *use* events in the world to bring about other events and that we do so in the light of both every day and scientific knowledge of the law-like regularities in the material world. Such knowledge, to reiterate, is clearly not part of the causal nexus; not the least because it *describes* the causal nexus and from the most general point of view. It is difficult to see how material causation could have given rise to the general notion of causation, or of requisitioning instances of types of causes to bring about specific effects – let alone general, invisible and abstract ones such as 'improving my cardiovascular health by going to the gym'. In short there is a cognitive space in which causes are identified, laws or simple correlations are observed, and causes and laws are exploited. This exploitation gets more explicit and complex and indirect as our actions are mediated through a multitude of technologies. Causes are plucked out of the buzz, blur, continuum (take your pick) of events by their relevance to a felt or anticipated need. There is, moreover, a lack of reciprocity. Though action and reaction are equal and opposite, the handles we use to realise our intentions do not use or handle us. The relationship is asymmetrical, non-reciprocal. Persons hammer; hammers do not 'person'.

This is the (undeniably real) space of our agency, of the operation of our free will. To deny this space – and to insist that we are totally absorbed in material nature as understood by objective physics – is to deny what is in front of our eyes: that we knowingly exploit laws and use events as keys to unlock complex paths to goals; and that there is a fundamental difference between law-driven or law-governed events on the one hand and law-exploiting actions. It is a matter of directly observed reality that we do use causes and do exploit laws and frequently do so not only deliberately but also very indirectly.

Actions moreover are irreducibly complex, being composed of subordinate parts of overarching elements that serve intermediate ends *en route* to various goals often specified only in very general terms (such as 'getting fit'). These elements are situated in a multitude of frames of reference that make sense of them and are the occasion for their occurrence: there is a succession of nested 'in-order-to's. The components of the action happen only because of the explicit purpose they serve. They occur for *reasons*.

The space of such reasons is itself located in a wider space: that of (future) possibility. It is this that makes sense of the idea of choice, and the exercise of choice, in voluntary action, and of a free agent who acts in one way but could act differently. Free agents can make choices because they envisage, explicitly entertain, a range of possibilities – often but not always expressed in words – to choose between and selectively realise. By contrast, the law-driven, causally closed material world does not contain possibilities: it has only actualities. At any moment it is what it is at that moment. Possibilities, by contrast, exist only so far as they are entertained by conscious beings. Free agents, then, are free ultimately because they can choose between possibilities they are capable of envisaging and can then use existing actualities as keys to realising one possibility rather than another. As we have seen, this may be very indirect indeed. The fear of future illness that makes sense of the cause-requisitioning travel to the gym, is motivated by an imagined future to which (at present) nothing corresponds in the material world. Indeed, the aim is to prevent that future from materialising.

The vast community of minds that is the reality in which human agents live – mediated by a multitude of sign systems, technologies and institutions – sustains endless parallel possible worlds alongside the actual material one. In that community, it is possible for an individual to connect a concept such as 'future ill health' (to which there is attached a vast body of knowledge and diagnostic and therapeutic and institutional procedures founded on it) with the concept of exercise-for-the-sake-of-its-physiological effects in a gym.

This brings me to something central to our freedom: tensed time. Agents and their free actions are steeped in tensed time: the explicit presence of our individual and collective pasts and futures and the present, the common now, that divides them. In the course of an action, the actor selects from the present that which is relevant to realising a particular future envisaged on the basis of an explicit past that itself feeds into the sense of the present and its future possibilities. The reference to 'past', 'present', and 'future' highlights how the realm of explicit possibility has temporal dimensions not found in the closed world of universal causation and physical laws.

Tense is an aspect of time that cannot be accommodated by physics because it has no part in the natural world in the absence of human consciousness. The past is no more there among the rocks and trees and bears than is 'last Wednesday' or 'ten years ago'. Tensed time is not in the fabric of the material world revealed to or by physics. As Einstein himself famously said (in a letter to the widow of his oldest friend Michele Besso):

Physicists know that the distinction between past, present and future is only a stubbornly persistent illusion.

Illusion or not, it has real power and makes us powerful. While explicitly entertained possibilities, intelligibility, and temporal depth or tensed time have no place in the material reality of the causally closed world revealed to science, they are indisputably real aspects of ordinary actions. No wonder the free will that is built on them also seems to have no place in the causally closed world. No wonder physicists and neuroscientists looking at the physical brain cannot find free agency and are, consequently, inclined to deny its reality. Picking out and requisitioning causes and exploiting the laws of nature – the very essence of voluntary action – is not itself reducible to a series of causes and yet it is undeniable that this is what we do all the time. We look temporally upstream and downstream, inferring causes from effects and seeing causes as instruments to bring about effects.

Actions, then, while they are causes of effects, are clustered causes that, uniquely, *use* causes: agents requisition causes – picked out of a range of events embedded in present circumstances – to bring about certain future ends.

ACTING FROM OUTSIDE: HOMO EX MACHINA

The use of the laws of nature to bend the world to our wishes is easier to understand if we appreciate firstly that more than one law may be operative at a given time and place; and secondly that we humans have collectively created an 'outside' from which we are able to align ourselves with one of those laws rather than another. The first point is made by John Stuart Mill in a posthumously published essay titled 'On Nature'.

Mill was concerned to reconcile his metaphysics with his passion for liberty. What point could there be in defending political liberty if it were true that, given that we are subject to the laws of nature, there are in fact no free agents? He acknowledged that, yes, our actions are in conformity to the laws of nature; but he denied that this meant that we in reality have no choices. At any given juncture, he argued, there is more than one law of nature operating. (This is the other side of the fact that no single law of nature is sufficiently specific to prescribe a singular, an actual event.) We are at liberty, therefore, to align ourselves with one law rather than another. By this means, we can use nature to achieve our chosen ends. This is how he puts it:

Though we cannot emancipate ourselves from the laws of nature as a whole, we can escape from any particular law of nature if we are able to withdraw ourselves from the circumstances in which it acts. Though we can do nothing except through laws of nature, we can use one law to counteract another.

We *utilize* the laws of nature by aligning ourselves with the one that leads to our goal.

We can illustrate Mill's idea with a trivial example: going to a park in order to enjoy slithering down a slide. The descent is courtesy of the laws of gravity but positioning ourselves to enjoy the descent is something else. Mummy has to agree to take us to the park and find the time to do so. The trip has to be organized, other things have to be fitted around it, there is a journey to the park, to the playground, and thence to the slide, guided by all sorts of know-how and know-that, and there is an ascent to the top of the slide. The slide itself has been erected in advance in order explicitly to utilize the laws of motion to give children pleasure: it is the standing possibility of the joy of safely succumbing to the gravitational field – by appointment. And using another law of nature – expressed in the resistance of the railings either side of the slide – will ensure that the descent does not end in tears.

This trivial example illustrates how our ways of acting, which involve knowledge as well as artefacts (which of course operate within the laws of nature), suborn nature to our own ends. As Mill said, quoting Francis Bacon, we 'obey nature so as to command her'. Our actions are not uncaused miracles: they go with the grain of causation. But we are able to step back into the great extra-natural space that is the human world and from there use material causes as handles or levers.

It is all about positioning ourselves. And we can regard much of our life as positioning ourselves, both literally and metaphorically, seeking out the situations in which we can exercise choice and maximise our chances of acting in accordance with our wishes. Practising, self-training, seeking learning opportunities – modes of behaviour which are unique to humans – are clearly dependent on a well-developed sense of tensed time. We can even train ourselves to be effective mechanisms, or automata, so that we can do things without thought that once we could not do deliberately. An example would be the capacity to respond instantaneously to catch a cricket ball flying off a bat. This ability to respond seemingly involuntarily, an action taking fractions of a second, is not the work of seconds: it has been cultivated in months and years spent practising, leading up to the time when the ball had to be caught.

This then is the 'outside of nature' from which we act on nature, utilise its laws, and make its events causes of outcomes we seek. It is not a real or material outside but a virtual one that enables us to use causes as if from outside the causal net. Its most impressive manifestations are in the technologies which incorporate our collective might. The human world is in part a great space of skills, technologies, modes of cooperation, and institutions, in which individually and collectively we are able to distance ourselves from the material circumstances which seem to define us. This is why we are *not* soluble fish dissolved by causes and laws in the material world but individuals and teams who engage with that world transformed into a substrate for our agency. We confront, we *face*, the world and we appropriate it as the theatre of lives that are actively *lived* as opposed to organic existence that is merely undergone.

This apartness is most clearly evident in vision, by means of which we are engaged with the world from a distance. Visual distance is subtler than mere physical separation. It is rooted in the fact that visual (and indeed other) perception is *about* that which is explicitly other than itself. The technical term for this 'aboutness' is *intentionality*. Vision is not, of course, enough; otherwise we might find ourselves committed to granting free will rather extensively in the animal kingdom. While intentionality may be present in other higher animals, in us humans, who are full-blown embodied subjects and not just organisms, it is elaborated in many ways. Explicit memory and anticipation, language and other symbolic systems which permit the pooling of our consciousness in the community of minds, all extend the scope of the aboutness in virtue of which we can engage with the world around us and yet not be immersed in it. Our connection with that world is thus not a straightforward causal wiring. The social character of conceptual thinking that may direct action, makes those actions irreducible to a mere effect of the properties of the human organism, necessary though the latter is for our agency.

The community of minds has been built up over many hundreds of thousands of years. It involves countless individuals who together maintain that virtual outside from which it is possible to operate upon the material world as a free agent. This outside is built up as a widening Space of Possibility, a first-person plural reality, constructed through the joined endeavours of the human race, and expanding since the first hominids first awoke to their own existence as subjects offset from nature, *facing* a world, that we do not face as isolated individuals, even when we are physically alone. Our joint attention to what is before us elaborates this public space, a fabric of common reality, that is woven out of billions of threads of human intercourse acknowledging and creating shared experiences.

This public sphere is above all a dense network of signs, of meant meanings, a 'semiosphere' of co-operative activity, rather than simply a biosphere, and a 'technosphere' of artefacts and techniques, in which we live and have our being beyond the material of our bodies. This is where we first elucidate the laws of nature and get them to work on our behalf. It is where we use our pooled outside and our pooled powers to 'step back' from nature and operate on the material world in accordance with our aims. This stepping back is the basis of the volition that pervades all our waking moments.

DETERMINISM'S LAST STAND

I hope by this stage that you are persuaded that it is all over for determinism and that we really can be free. That the apparently fundamental difference between an involuntary event such as falling down the stairs, and a voluntary action such as going to the gym to postpone future ill health, corresponds to a reality. And that there is a solid difference between a life that is actively lived and an existence that is merely endured. But determinists don't give up without a fight, even if (according to the belief they are defending) their fight is merely an expression of unchosen physical and biological forces.

Here are some of their objections:

Even Very Complex Actions May be Programmed

Think of a swallow going back to the same nesting grounds each year, undertaking a 5,000-mile journey, made of hundreds of thousands of wing beats and doing it in the face of buffeting winds blowing it on and off course. The goal is relatively specific and yet the journey, extended over considerable time, is programmed.

Are we going to concede that swallows have free will as we do, on the grounds that the hundreds of thousands of movements that constitutes their migration would have a negligible probability of occurring by chance? And if not, why not? Does this heroic journey not depend on a sustained intention that requisitions movements? The answer is No – for two reasons. First, the journey can be steered by something corresponding to inner GPS which does not require the bird to be aware of the relationship between its present position and the destination in order to keep it on, or restore it to, its course. We could imagine something analogous to a robotic car directed in the same way by a satnav which can indeed be programmed and the programme can include course corrections. Secondly – and this is a connected point – it seems unlikely, from what we know about other aspects of a swallow's consciousness reflected in other behaviour, that it chooses its destination (as we would choose a holiday) on the basis of weighing of pros and cons, or indeed even envisages the place it is headed for. The swallow is, what is more (to mix my metaphors) a one-trick pony. By contrast, our human repertoire of actions is limitless and personalised, not general to my species. Your vast bag of tricks, reader, is significantly different from mine and the acquisition and use of them is rooted in a personal history that is available to you. Moreover, at any given time, I – as do you – mobilise a *multitude* of interwoven bespoke tricks directed towards singular goals. None of the people going to a lecture is attending exactly for the same purpose or has arrived by the same volitional route. Like other actions, it makes sense only in relation to a personal history; and, in the journey from start to completion, attendees may mount and dismount from a multitude of other complex actions related to immediate, medium-term and long-term goals.

Our Actions are the Effects of Inner Causes

The foregoing argument also disposes of the idea that human actions are unfree because pushed from behind by biologically or culturally determined programmes, rather than drawn from the front towards explicit goals. Even if such push 'forces' were customised to each individual, having been shaped by a unique history, so that the acts arising out of them were expressive of our self, determinists would still argue that they must be unchosen. Against this argument, it is necessary only to point out that general motives, instincts, tropisms, cultural conditioning etc. would not deliver us to singular goals, situated in a space of reasons, a network of 'in-order-to' unless they were evident to us, and accepted by us. That is why the self out of which we act cannot be reduced to a mere set of states buried in the past, acting upon the present as if they were external forces or influences. We could not shape our lives as we manifestly do if we were simply in the grip of unconscious and general forces, even ones inflected by our singular lives. Unlike ordinary actions, pro-grammed behaviour does not require the explicit co-operation or informed consent of the behaver.

Our Freedom is Limited and Contingent

One thing is certainly true: the extent to which we can freely pursue our own ends is dependent on many things over which we have no control. These include the century, country, socio-economic class and other circumstances in which we were born and our health (particularly our mental health). Beyond quite narrow certain limits, we are not free to choose the degree to which we are free. Not infrequently we are bound by habits acquired involuntarily, and are sometimes pris-oners of the consequences of our free choices. Those of us who are lucky enough to shape our own lives more than others – who may have been terrorised, impris-oned, oppressed, starved, denied education – cannot take credit for what is, after all, luck. Our freedom may be all but terminated by a head injury or by dementia picking apart the connectedness out of which our abil-ity to achieve clearly conceived, personally elected ends grows. All of this is true. And it is equally true that we are not ultimately self-caused. We did not choose to be born and many of our characteristics are givens.

None of this removes the possibility, or dem-onstrates the unreality, of freedom for two reasons. Firstly, recognising that some are freer than others, or we are freer at some times or in some circumstances, is an indirect acknowledgement of the fact that we are free to at least some degree and at some times; or if this seems too generous, that freedom itself is possible. We cannot have more or less freedom without there being freedom: accidentally falling down the stairs highlights the voluntary nature of walking down them in order to set out to London to chair a meeting. In contrast, determinism does not permit even circumscribed freedom. Secondly, to say that we can be free only if we had no givens in our lives – body, health, experiences, character, circumstances – would be to make freedom empty. Without a starter pack of 'the given' as it were – the most important one being that one had been given a life to live – there would be nothing to be free from, about, or for. Freedom is making something of, and contributing to shaping, the givens of one's life. Freedom grows out of a self – selfhood and freedom develop in parallel – and the self has to be built on something. For a free act to be expressive of a self, there has to be a self for it to express.

Our Sense of Being Free is Adaptive Illusion

If the laws of physical nature were the whole story about what happens even in human life, it would be reasonable to ask by what cause a part of the causally closed world – namely us human beings – came to the conclusion that it was part of a causally closed world;

by what laws it arrived at an understanding of the laws of nature, and learned how to exploit them – most strikingly in everyday technology; and, more specifically, by what causes or laws those who feel they are free, arrived at this supposed illusion.

Determinists have an answer even to this challenge. Rita Carter, a brilliant populariser of neuroscience, has offered an explanation in Darwinian terms (in *Mapping the Mind*):

The illusion of free will is deeply ingrained precisely because it prevents us from falling into a suicidally fatalistic state of mind – it is one of the brain's most powerful aids to survival.

Claiming that the illusion of freedom carries evolutionary benefits on the grounds that assuming responsibility for our actions promotes survival by making us feel more powerful (and even behave more ethically) is implausible for many reasons. How did a part of the causal network benefit by *deluding* itself that it was controlling other parts? Why should magic thinking and imagining that we are *doing* things that were going to happen anyway actually deflect the course of events (by altering our behaviour) given that nothing else does? Of course – and this is the key point – if it *did* deflect the course of events, then we are in fact free, not merely subject to the illusion of freedom. The argument from illusion undermines itself.

CONCLUSION

And so my quarrel with my fifteen-year-old self – or rather his present day proxies – reaches its conclusion. We have seen how a creature such as a human being who *faces* the world – who faces the physical world from within shared and individual human worlds – can be a true originator of events in the material world. We have seen also how those events are expressive not of his or her present physical state but of a self steeped in tensed time, in a private history: they are self-expressive. We have seen how, acting from the virtual outside of the human world, we can utilise causes and take advantage of laws to bring about ends we desire. And we have seen, finally, how through envisaging possibilities, and indeed proposing an entire world of possibilities, we have genuine choice rather than simply being pushed down pre-determined pathways.

Those who doubt that we can individually or collectively affect the course of the history of our part of the universe, in ways not envisaged in the laws of motion or the unwilled properties of living matter, should open their eyes and look at what we humans have achieved. We have created a human world so extensive as virtually at times to conceal the natural one. As was said of Christopher Wren, '*Si monumentum requiris, circumspice*': if you seek His monument, look about you. Looking about us, we see evidence of human beings as the originators of an entire extra-natural reality.

89

Cathedrals were built using the laws of nature but they are not, like trees and mountains, an uninflected expression of the laws of nature. And as collective self-expression, unlike coral reefs and anthills, they had to be intended, and brought into being as much by discussion as by the push and pull of mechanical effort.

The 'artefactscapes' of the cities which cover the surface of the earth with man-made objects (to the extent that the present epoch of the planet has been designated the Anthropocene), the human institutions to which we relate for so much of our lives, and the social facts and preoccupations that fill our waking hours, to which there is nothing corresponding in nature – these are eloquent testimony to how, collectively at least, we deflect the course of events; and how beyond this we build new worlds, platforms from which we are able to operate within a space outside of the material world construed according to the laws of physics. There is a story parallel to unfolding nature: it is human history.

From our gestures, through spoken, and ultimately written, language, and a vast chest of tools, we get a stronger purchase on the natural world from an ever more expansive outside built up by successive generations comprised at first of thousands, then of millions and ultimately of billions, of people. To our ancestors, our contemporaries, and our own efforts we owe our considerable margin of freedom. We found the world not ordered according to our needs and wishes and started re-ordering it.

By now, alas, I suspect that the ghost of Dr Johnson has long lost patience with me. And well he might. He knows that nobody really believes we are not free. Why, if we were not free, or did not believe we were, would we bother arguing that we are? What would we hope to change? Persuading another by argument that she is not free, after all, is a sophisticated, if self-refuting, exercise of free will. I hope, by contrast, I have persuaded the reader of the opposite. 'We *know* our will is free,' Johnson said, 'and *there's* an end on it.'

Anyone who wishes to dispute this is, of course, free to do so.

4

– Lord Howe's Wicked Dream –

A Report from an Undeveloping Country

All action weakens contemplation. – Plotinus

I could never get over some queasiness from indulging in
strident public rhetoric which took me further and further
away from my own interior musing, in which skepticism,
uncertainty, and ambivalence play large parts.
– Phillip Lopate

In future the NHS will be a state insurance provider
and not a state deliverer . . . and the NHS will be
shown no mercy.
– Mark Britnell

There is an apocryphal story of a poet who is said
to have greeted the declaration of hostilities in
September 1939 with a cry of frustration: 'I have spent
over a decade learning how to use a semi-colon and
now a bloody war breaks out!' While not entirely sym-
pathetic to the egocentric writer, I felt a similar frustration when, from 2010 onwards, I was increasingly
distracted from various writing projects that had been
on the stocks for many years, and instead got caught
up in politics. I found myself spending hours on the
pavements of Stockport, Cheshire, talking to reluctant
interlocutors in frequently unattractive weather, trying

to persuade people to sign petitions, helping to write and distribute leaflets, and composing long letters to our local MP. All of which variously exasperated, depressed and bored me witless. I had exchanged crafting paragraphs in privacy and solitude for publicly shouting slogans in ragged chorus.

Though hardly comparable to the battle for civilization that had interrupted the poet, the cause that pitched me on to the streets was far from trivial: an ideologically motivated assault on the NHS by the Tories and unopposed by their Liberal-Democrat fellow-travellers. It was, and remains, a major threat to the health of my fellow citizens. As an ex-physician this was not something I could ignore.

Most of my waking consciousness for nearly forty years had been occupied by my life as a doctor: clinical practice, teaching and research, and developing medical services meant almost as much to me as my family. For several decades writing books was an intermittent aspiration. I was aware also that being healthy is for most of us a necessary condition of taking philosophical problems seriously and I had no reason to assume that my fellow citizens were any different in this respect. I am not sufficiently self-deceived to believe that I would think with any enthusiasm if I were in pain. To adapt Berthold Brecht's 'First grub, then ethics', I would suggest 'First analgesia, then metaphysics'.

Readers from outside of my Small Island might think that this story is a rather parochial affair of little significance beyond the shores of the UK. You would be mistaken. The neo-liberalism that is threatening the welfare of UK citizens and undermining its democratic processes is at work throughout the globe. The forces that are destroying the British National Health Service (NHS) are those that in the USA are ensuring that the interests of Big Business triumph over the medical needs of the vast majority of the people, such that attempts to move towards a healthcare system that does not rip off and ruin those who are foolish enough to fall ill, are frustrated at every turn.

Needless to say, those of us who raised the alarm about what the politicians were up to were accused of scare-mongering but increasingly what we tannoyed to the largely indifferent shoppers of Stockport has proved to be truth-mongering. Truth, however, has become so scarce that speaking it seems at best eccentric. And this is the cue for a note on nomenclature.

There are some politicians where the flow of lies is so seamless that it is impossible to count them, never mind challenge them. Since I am not sufficiently crooked to have amassed a large enough fortune to defend myself against libel actions, however unjust, I have to be careful in my choice of language. In many cases, 'not true' means 'barefaced lie'. In some instances, this will be obvious, as when David Cameron says that he will protect child benefit, the NHS, the poor and the vulnerable, and then does the opposite. Or when Jeremy Hunt (present Secretary of State for Health) falsely claims that the 2012 'reforms' of the NHS have saved the service £2,000,000,000 that has been put back into front-line services, or that privatisation of healthcare is not happening and not only is it not happening but that it's the GPs that are doing it. Or . . . Well you get the picture. When you see the word 'untruth' be alert to the probability of a lie.

The story so far as I was concerned began with a cloud no bigger than a man's hand: a government White Paper, published in June 2010, six weeks after the Coalition between the Tories and Liberal Democrats had been formed, putatively to save the country from a financial crisis. The document was called 'Equity and Excellence: Liberating the NHS' and was the brainchild of one Andrew Lansley who had been shadow Secretary of State for Health since 2005.

During his long years in opposition Lansley had conceived a plan of such cunning that, as Blackadder might have said, if you had put a tail on it you could have made it Professor of Cunning at the University of Oxford. Hidden in its many pages of leaden prose, empty rhetoric, and whopping untruths, there was a solution to a conundrum that had exercised the Tories since the early 1980s: namely, how to fulfil a dream, first articulated in cabinet by the then Chancellor of the Exchequer, Geoffrey Howe, of ending 'the state provision of healthcare, so that medical facilities would be privately owned and run and those seeking health-care would be required to pay for it'.

The 1982 dream remained a dream because it was overwhelmingly opposed by the electorate. (And still is: 84 per cent of them in the most recent poll.) It was not, however, allowed to die. In 1988, Oliver Letwin and John Redwood, two prominent and influential right wing Tories, published *Privatising the Universe.* (Letwin was hardly disinterested – he has been an executive director of an investment company specialising in healthcare). The book inspired the first major step in pulling the NHS apart: the introduction in 1990 of what was called an 'internal market'.

NHS purchasers of healthcare (later called commissioners) would be separated from providers (such as hospitals) also in the NHS and the latter would compete with each other for what was now to be seen as 'business'. Enabling the NHS to compete with itself vastly increased bureaucracy and transaction costs. Putting together business cases, tendering for business, monitoring the delivery of contracts and so on consumed monstrous quantities of resources and clinical and managerial time. It also destabilised many of the public institutions responsible for providing care. It was a flying start.

To move decisively in the direction of Howe's dream, however, it was necessary to expose the NHS to external competition from those benefactors of mankind, the private healthcare providers. Successive Labour administrations between 1997 and 2010 put more publicly provided healthcare out to private tender, something of which the arch-privatisers in the Tory opposition greatly approved. The proportion of NHS business that was privately provided, however, remained less than five per cent. Something more radical had to be done in order to fulfil Letwin's 2005 boast that, within five years of a Tory government, the NHS (which he described as 'Stalinist') would not exist. How could the sixty-year nightmare of publicly provided, publicly funded, universal healthcare, free at the point of need to all, irrespective of means, finally be terminated?

Enter Mr Lansley with his White Paper. The paper started with certain premises: the NHS was inefficient; it was bureaucratic; it delivered poor care; and it was not democratically accountable. This would all be corrected by a central idea. Commissioning – the decision as to who gets what healthcare and who provides it – would be carried out by local Clinical Commissioning Groups (CCGs) led by GP's and the latter would respond to the wishes, views, and needs of patients. The democratic deficit in a 'monolithic', 'Stalinist' NHS would be healed. The mantra (supposedly voiced by a patient) 'No decision about me without me' would be the guiding principle of future public provision.

That all sounded very good. However, it was actively misleading. The premises on which the White Paper was built were false – something to which I shall return. More importantly, this was a smokescreen to cover the real purpose of the proposed 'reforms'. Buried in the waffle were three important principles. The first was that the Secretary of State for Health should no longer be responsible for providing comprehensive healthcare. This was the key towards ending government accountability for the NHS and the service it provided: '"Not my job gov", government' was presented as an advance in local democracy. The second was that, with some exceptions, all contracts for services would have to be put out to competitive tender. And finally, all providers would have to become independent businesses (or Foundation Trusts). They could earn up to 49 per cent of their income from private patients. What is more, they were no longer required to provide across-the-board services.

What attracted most attention when The White Paper was published was that it envisaged a massive top-down reorganisation – only a few weeks after the partners to the Coalition had promised to the electorate that there would be no top-down re-organisation of the NHS. The then CEO of the NHS said it was the biggest in its history and so large 'it could be seen from outer space'. No wonder the Tories had forbidden Lansley from talking about his cunning plan before the election because, as Michael Portillo, a former Tory minister said, 'they would not have got elected'. They had, in short, lied, so that Geoffrey Howe's dream could be imposed without electoral consent. The Liberal-Democrats trotted along behind because they were hungry for office. 'All power corrupts,' Lord Acton said; and, we might add, 'so do years of impotence'.

The White Paper was moulded into a parliament-ary Bill. At over three hundred pages it was three times as long as the document that established the NHS. After a rocky journey through the two chambers, and agonisingly slow progress – though greatly assisted by the eloquence of unscrupulous parliamentarians with a personal interest in private health businesses and a hope of getting a share of the action – the Bill received Royal Assent as the Health and Social Care Act (HSCA) in March 2012. It was implemented in April 2013.

Among the Bill's most assiduous, indeed tireless, supporters was another ennobled Howe: hereditary peer Earl Howe. The tireless Earl's silver tongue may justifiably be credited with applying the KY jelly to ease the passage of Lansley's Semtex suppository into the rear of the NHS, a public service so long loathed by the Tories. Earl Howe ensured that nothing of real substance in the Bill was changed by the time it reached the statute book.

The NHS was ready for sale.

A BLAZING ROW WITH EDMUND BURKE

At the end of 2012, a group of us had established Stockport NHS Watch to hold our local Clinical Com-missioning Group (CCG) to account and to campaign for the repeal of the Lansley's Act. We spent a lot of time on the streets. We had some low-altitude highs

– as when we managed to persuade our local MP to be photographed for that organ of record *The Stockport Express and Advertiser* receiving a petition (3,000 signatures no less) – and many lows. It was chastening being on the pavement, seen as a minor nuisance (cf. Jehovah's Witnesses) interrupting busy people on busy days; being dismissed as wrong or naïve; or simply ignored or brushed aside. As an academic used to addressing audiences that had the courtesy at least to simulate attention, I felt distinctly disempowered.

Such woes are low grade compared with those of my fellow citizens who (in increasing numbers) have to beg to live, are going hungry, or living in filthy accommodation at the mercy of an unscrupulous landlord. I mention them only as a background to an event that took place some six months after Lansley's Monster (as the *British Medical Journal* called it) got to work. With several thousand others, we joined The Darlington Mums on the last leg of their *March for the NHS* from Jarrow to London. I was deeply touched by this raggle-taggle army (parading near the Department of Health where much of the dirty work has been done) and by the spectacle of people willing to stand up for values unknown to our political masters and the money men who run them. But I also felt a crushing sense of impotence. The City and neo-liberal privatisers were not there to argue their case. They didn't need to: that case was proceeding smoothly. They let the money do the talking. We were pitchforks against the invisible machine guns of the hedge fund managers who (contrary to Shelley's famous assertion about poets) are the unacknowledged legislators of the world.

By the time we entered Trafalgar Square (for some great speeches – fellow citizen of Stockport Owen Jones was magnificent), I was having a blazing argument. My interlocutor was none other than Edmund Burke, the conservative political philosopher who is a darling of some sections of the Tory party and had been identified as the Godfather of the idea of Cameron's Big Society. The Big Society is opposed to the Big Government. One passage from Burke's *Reflections on the Revolution in France* is endlessly quoted:

To love the little platoons we belong to in society is the first principle ... of public affections. It is the first link in the series by which we proceed toward a love to our country and to mankind.

The Darlington Mums seemed to me a paradigm of the little platoons: an association formed to serve a common cause of defending something they valued and which expressed their shared values. But faced with a government that used the rhetoric of 'getting the state off people's backs' in order to pave the way for privatisation of the public sphere (against the will of the people), the Darlo mums had little chance of changing things.

The self-interested dogma that unfettered markets

and the privatisation of everything would deliver the best outcome for all was dominating the thinking of the political class, notwithstanding the catastrophe of 2007–8, and the dismal results of other privatisations (gas, electricity, railways). Money talks and its voice drowns out all others: the lobbyists lunching with venal legislators have 'a quiet word' and the deal is clinched. Brrr!

Burke's opposition to top-down organisation of society in favour of grass roots, local action, was fashioned in the wake of events in France that he meditated on so brilliantly in his *Reflections.* He saw that trying to build up society from scratch according to explicit, rational principles would inevitably lead to disaster. He was right; but his ideas have been hi-jacked by those who loath collective action of any sort, particularly if it involves them paying taxes. Hence Big Society rather than Big Government. The breaking up of the NHS was thus presented as a liberation of the people from a 'monolithic, Stalinist' organisation. The little platoons disagreed. The NHS represents some of our most fundamental values: a decency that acknowledges that we should share the risks that come from the lottery of life. Hence the commitment to publicly provided, universal healthcare, free at the point of need; and to seeing illness as a shared responsibility rather than a business opportunity.

Needless to say, back on the streets of Stockport the conversation was rarely of political philosophy and our leaflets were not always well-received, as this epistle that popped through our letterbox just before the May 2015 election suggested:

Dear Mr Tallis

I have just received the latest flyer from Stockport NHS Watch.

When I need a sad failed bank clerk to spew out their uninformed gobshite I'll ask you.

'Galloping privatisation'. Bring it on. Make nurses work harder and more efficiently. Charge the obese, lazy scroungers who clog up the system for their treatment.

But no lets (sic) just fucking moan about making improvements. Lets (sic) put up VAT to 50% to pay to make the NHS bigger and less efficient.

You are a thick, irrelevant cunt.

I intend to put a lot of dog shit through your letterbox over the coming weeks.

Enjoy!

THINGS I WANTED TO HAVE BEEN ABLE TO SAY ON THE PAVEMENT

A professor without PowerPoint is a sad creature. So let's get out of the rain into a quiet, warm place. I would like to crave your indulgence for a short address on Mr Lansley's Health and Social Care Act, on the untruths that made the case for it, and on some of its consequences.

The premise behind Mr Lansley's radical reforms was that the NHS was a basket case. This was untrue. There were serious problems – as there are with all health systems – but international comparisons in 2011 and 2014 (before the HSCA had had time to do its work) carried out by the New York based think tank The Commonwealth Fund told a different story. The 2014 comparison, based on data gathered roughly while Lansley's Bill was passing through parliament, compared healthcare in eleven industrialised countries: Australia, Canada, France, Germany, Netherlands, New Zealand, Norway, Sweden, Switzerland, UK, USA. Guess what? The NHS was top for quality of care, access, safety, value for money, and overall. The USA (which had 2.5 times as much expenditure on healthcare per head) was ranked bottom. The cornerstone of Lansley's case for his changes was therefore a lie. What is more, as the Centre for Health Economics in York discovered, increase in NHS productivity in the years leading up to Lansley had outstripped that of the national economy by a country mile. At the same time the quality and outcome of care had continued to improve.

The second declared reason for the HSCA was to bring patients and GPs to the centre of decision-making in the NHS. In fact, (and not by oversight) it has had the opposite effect: patients' watchdogs are toothless, the public voice is virtually silenced, and a survey of GPs a year after the Act went live revealed that the majority now had a lesser role in determining the shape of local services and who provided them. The hugely important strategic decision to create a single merged health and social care budget in Greater Manchester in 2015 was sprung upon the populace and most of their elected representatives as a complete surprise. It now makes its deliberations behind doors that remain stubbornly closed. As for Stockport NHS Watch, it met a wall of silence when it dug too deep; that is to say to the level that mattered.

Lansley also told us that the HSCA would reduce bureaucracy – as signalled in the subtitle of the White Paper 'Liberating the NHS'. Result? In 2011 there were 160 bodies managing and regulating the NHS; by 2014 there were 443. Much of this was devoted to running the auction of bits of the service. The introduction of, in succession, the internal (1990) and external (2013) markets increased administrative (commissioning and billing) costs from 5 per cent in 1989 to 16 per cent of the NHS overall budget in 2014. Just getting the NHS to compete with *itself* was already, by 2010, costing billions of pounds – rather a lot of doctors, nurses, and hip replacements. The NHS market has been justly described as 'an unaffordable ideological luxury'. But when ideology is at stake neither expense nor truth should be spared.

So what was Lansley's Act *really* about? The answer has been well trailed in this essay: Lord Howe's 1983 dream of opening up the NHS to the market. More precisely, selling it off piece by piece. While the other Howe, Earl Howe, told parliament in 2011 that 'The Bill does not do anything that may or could lead to the privatisation of the NHS' he said something different when speaking over the canapés at a swish Lang Buisson Private Healthcare Forum. The NHS reforms, he said, presented 'huge opportunities for the private sector' though 'the NHS will not give up their patients easily'.

And so it came to pass.

Between 2012 and 2014 (which included only one year in which the HSCA was live), the proportion of the NHS put out to private sector increased by 40 per cent and a third of contracts had gone to private bidders. By the first part of 2015, the pace was quickening. In the months running up to the May Election, Capita had been awarded a multi-billion-pound contract to oversee NHS commissioning, a £700 million contract had gone to a private consortium for elective surgery and £280 million for an 'Improving Lives' package in East Staffordshire. A whopping £1.2 billion contract for cancer and end-of-life care came to light only when a key document was leaked to the press and the sell-off was temporarily halted. It is still being argued over. (One of the early bidders was Lockheed, maker of Hell-fire missiles. Whether they offered to make care of the dying cheaper by making it shorter is not clear.) In 2015–16, 37 per cent of £6 billion worth of NHS clinical contracts went to the private sector, many of them concealing their nature by operating under the NHS logo.

Not exactly the 'galloping privatisation' of our leaflet; but the direction of travel was set and the end point was clear. But should we not echo our dog dirt-promising correspondent and say 'Bring it on!'? Surely the private sector is cheaper, more innovative, and the disciplines of the market will drive the continuous improvement that a publicly run organisation would obstruct? Think Microsoft, think Apple, think . . .

Well, think . . . More importantly *look* and you will see sixty-five or more years of constant clinician-driven innovation within the NHS, improvements in treatments and ways of delivering them, lateral and frontal thinking, often subsequently drawn upon, indeed parasitized by the private sector. And all of this had been achieved in the face of chronic underfunding and constant reorganisation by a succession of ministers eager to make their mark *en route* to one of the more attractive offices of state.

Again and again on the streets I was told, by those who stopped to talk, that it didn't matter who provided health care – public bodies or private multinationals – so long as it was free at the point of need. Oh yes, it does matter. There are many reasons for anticipating that in principle a privatised service would deliver less care for more money.

The most important is that a full-blown health market replaces cooperation for the benefit of patients as the guiding principle with competition for the benefit of shareholders. When it comes to examples, I am spoiled for choice but one sticks in my mind and indeed my throat. In 2013, two hospital trusts in the south of England decided to work more closely to-gether, to save money and to offer a much-improved patient service including a 24/7 consultant presence in Accident and Emergency. The plan was enthusias-tically supported by clinicians, local politicians, and most importantly patients. It was about to go forward when the local private hospital cried foul at what they saw as anti-competitive practice and a threat to their 'business model' and hence to their income. Imple-mentation ground to a halt. The subsequent court bat-tle cost huge fees, wasted a vast quantity of clinician and managerial time, and put one of the trusts into serious debt. The crucial improvements in patient care were obstructed. Competition lawyers not clinicians had made a crucial decision about the way care would be delivered. The episode put the frighteners nation-ally on commissioners who were reluctant to risk any repetition. Cooperation was the new 'c' word.

The primary responsibility of healthcare business-es, their fiduciary duty, is to maximise profits, and not the overall health either of individuals or of popula-tions. Privatisation also means that taxpayers' money diverted from healthcare into profits may (as in the case of the top six private companies providing NHS care) be parked offshore, out of the reach of the tax-man who would want to use them to support public services such as the NHS. This would also deny the nation the boost to the economy from investment in public services – the so-called multiplier effect, first described by John Maynard Keynes. Which makes it deeply disappointing that commissioners are now forbidden to insist that successful private bidders for NHS contracts should be restricted to companies that actually pay taxes on their profits because this would be challenged by lawyers as 'discriminatory'. Privatised healthcare is fragmented into separate elements run by different for-profit organisations that have no interest in working together, though there has never been a time when, with a largely elderly patient population who need closely integrated services, this been more important. There is the obvious disruptive effect of fixed term contracts going to a succession of providers, with services being stopped and started. Privatisation will also have an impact on the ethos of clinical staff: doctors and nurses change from public servants for whom the needs of patients are paramount into loyal company men and women keen, like their bosses, to shift as much product as possible. Professional covenants are replaced by hard-headed contractual obligations. While many ill people who have the wrong insurance package will be denied the care they do need, the well-insured will be flogged profitable treatments they don't.

I have already mentioned the billions squandered in running bidding for services and in increased transaction costs. (Administration accounts for 31 per cent of health expenditure in USA.) As competitive organisations, private firms operate behind a veil of secrecy: public accountability will be buried under 'commercial confidentiality' that trumps public interest. Unlike the NHS, private providers are not obliged to respond to Freedom of Information requests, or to report safety incidents and their level of performance. And last (but by no means least to a one-time medical teacher and researcher such as myself), the privateers have neither the commitment nor the obligation to support training, education, or research; in short to the future of healthcare.

These are the reasons in principle why privatisation is potentially disastrous but have they been born out in practice? The international comparisons have already been alluded to, with the most marketised system, the United States, producing the worst results for patients at the greatest expense – roughly twice the UK cost per head of population. The burden of illness is compounded by the prospect of ruin. Just under a million or 62 per cent of all US bankruptcies in 2014 were due to medical bills. Four fifths of those who were bankrupted as a result of falling ill were fully insured but were foolish enough to have had bodies that did not read the small print and avoid the diseases which would be orphaned by said small print.

The evidence is already growing for the malign effects of privatisation in the UK, giving early warning as to how things will be when the healthcare multinationals are allowed to dominate the NHS. A direct comparison found that the GP practices taken over by private providers (Virgin alone runs 358 surgeries) performed worse than traditional practices in fifteen out of seventeen performance indicators even when adjustments had been made for the characteristics of the population served. Ditto ambulance services. But there are worse things happening than minor deterioration of services. Private providers have picked up and put down GP surgeries, out-of-hours cover, and ambulance transport, often dropping them from their portfolios at very short notice in response to mounting complaints, leaving patients stranded. A significant number of patients are transferred as emergencies from private outfits to the NHS. The NHS is there to pick up the pieces when profitable elective surgery and other nice little earners go wrong.

The most spectacular failure was Hinchingbrooke Hospital which Circle took over, for a 10-year contract, with a great fanfare of trumpets. Circle were going to transform clinical services and at the same time solve the hospital's financial problems. Three years later, in advance of a very critical report on patient care and in the face of losses their shareholders would not tolerate, they walked away from the contract, leaving the hospital high and dry. They had other, more profitable fish to fry.

Expensive and time-consuming competitive tendering has brought problems of its own, irrespective of the choice of preferred bidder. In Cambridge an NHS consortium joined the auction for older persons' services, with private and public providers beating each other down on price, in a process that was largely secret. Three healthcare multinationals withdrew when they saw that the profit margin would be small or non-existent. An NHS consortium won the £800 million five-year contract. It proved a Pyrrhic victory and within eight months the partners had to declare that they could not continue delivering agreed services at the agreed price. The tendering process cost at least £1,000,000 – yes, £1,000,000 – and countless hours of the time of clinicians and managers. The services are in crisis.

So much for the benefits of privatisation. Thank you for your attention.

FROM MR LANSLEY'S SWIVEL EYES TO MR HUNT'S WAGGED FINGER

Our ambition should be to break down the barriers
between private and public provision, in effect
denationalising the provision of healthcare in Britain.
– Jeremy Hunt, 2005

It was soon obvious even to its supporters that HSCA was a disaster. The very fact that the NHS had kept going in the face of this, the nth reorganisation in a very few years and the biggest in NHS history, was a tribute to the incredible robustness of the service and the fierce commitment of those working in it. The latter had had to achieve what in the world of computing would be equivalent to writing files on a disc while it was being reformatted. In November 2014 David Cameron admitted that he had not understood Lansley's ideas (nor had the civil servants in the Department of Health required to transmit them) and that the HSCA was the 'biggest mistake' his party had made in government.

The competition for that accolade might seem fierce. But it wasn't just a mistake of course. It was a broken promise ('no more top-down reorganisations'). And Cameron's admission was disingenuous for another reason. Though disastrous for the service, Lansley's Act was already starting to deliver the privatisation it was designed to promote. The shake-up had, however, cost between £2.5 and £3 billion pounds, in addition to diverting immeasurable quantities of clinical attention from patient care, as doctors and others tried to understand it and make it work. It had resulted in a structure that was declared by the *Economist* to be 'in a special circle of bureaucratic Hell'. Mr Lansley, the swivel-eyed visionary behind it, had been demoted to Speaker of the House of Commons and there was a new Secretary of State for Health: Jeremy Hunt. He was just the man for the job.

It was not only his seemingly calm demeanour that suited him for taking over the helm at the

Department of Health when the NHS was in the grip of a government-inflicted crisis. Nor his ability to spin or find facts as the occasion demanded – as when he claimed that Lansley's 'reforms' were generating £2 billion pounds' saving a year which were available for front-line care. His most important qualification may have been his apparent aversion to the values implicit in public service, particularly as expressed in the state provision of medical care.

Hunt's contempt for the NHS had been spelled out in *Direct Democracy*, a volume which he had co-authored, in which he had asserted that the organisation was 'irrelevant to the 21st century'. In 2005, and again in 2008, he called for the de-nationalisation of the NHS and for a USA-style insurance scheme – and we know how well that works. His co-author was MEP Daniel Hannan, who called the NHS 'a 60-year mistake' and 'no longer relevant to the 21st century'. He claimed absurdly that by 2010 it would be the most expensive health service in the world.

Why did the new Secretary of State for (in practice *against*) Health dislike the NHS so much? This could not be on the basis of the effectiveness and efficacy of the NHS compared with other health systems as the professorial lecture to which you have just been subjected has demonstrated. Or was he unfamiliar with the facts? It is easy to underestimate a minister's ignorance of his portfolio but even that doesn't seem to be the full explanation. Could it be that he did not *get* an institution built on the ideal of a nation that is a true community of individuals, motivated by concern for their fellow citizens, and informed by the noble principle of sharing risks in facing the lottery of life and death, of health and sickness? Was there (to borrow Oscar Wilde's image) a touch of Caliban's rage at not seeing his own face in a glass and of having to deal with people who had values he did not share and who in their daily life carried responsibilities and deployed skills he could not imagine? Could it be that his seeming contempt for the NHS, in short, was not on the basis of what it did but on account of what it stood for? The fact that it was more successful than any other healthcare system could only make him loath it more.

This is pure speculation but, as he is such an important player and because he is in many respects an exemplar, it is worth pursuing this further and – at the risk of seeming to stoop to *ad hominem* attacks – to reflect on his CV. The shilling life – namely, Wikipedia – tells you all you need to know and it is terrifyingly relevant to the probable fate of the NHS. It also shows how, if the circumstances are right, the actions of a man who is an existential featherweight can cause long-lasting and profound damage.

After leaving university, Mr Hunt established a marmalade exporting business that failed. This may not have diminished his affection for sugary products. As Health Secretary he resisted calls from public health experts to support a sugar tax, a step that had been shown to be likely to have a significant impact on the current epidemic of obesity and consequently the health of the nation. (It was eventually introduced without any evidence of enthusiasm on his part.) Following the marmalade debacle, he moved to something less sticky and established, first of all, an IT PR company and then Hotcourses, an agency that lists courses for people who want to improve their work prospects or to follow a hobby. Whether or not his product had much to offer in the age of the internet, it made Mr Hunt a wealthy man and so freed him to enter politics. Being a millionaire did not discourage him from over-claiming on his parliamentary expenses or from avoiding £100,000 tax (the kind of stuff that pays for the NHS) by means of extremely fancy footwork that the *Daily Telegraph* (not a Marxist organ) thought worth reporting as an example of the 'aggressive' tax avoidance of which the Prime Minister and his colleague the Chancellor might disapprove. His seeming to cosy up to the Murdoch empire over the sale of the remainder of BSkyB when he, as Culture, Media and Sport secretary, had a quasi-judicial oversight suggested where his sympathies might lie. His preference for the private sector in his disastrous decision to hire G4S to oversee security at the London Olympics, with the result that the army had to be called in, might have given another clue. And his support for homoeopathy – the medical equivalent of dehydrated water and which a recent study showed to be effective in none of the 68 conditions in which it has been properly tested – reflected the cognitive bent of a man whose first success was in PR where spin is king and evidence an unwelcome guest. It has earned him the soubriquet (from Jonathan Pie) of 'Mystic 'unt'.

All of which indicates the enormity of the gulf between those who work in the NHS and the man who had a statutory but now arm's length responsibility for it. He has passed most of his adult life in a world where the aim is to sell as much product as possible and to maximise the profit margin. This is a long way from the ideals of a vocation, rooted in a rigorous education in the science and evidence-based practice of medical care. Sitting up all night worrying about a patient, doing the right thing for its own sake, would also look very odd in the free market world where he had made his millions.

In the light of this CV, it is easier to understand his crass and destructive approach to his duties as Secretary of State for Health. Even so, the allocation of causation between incompetence and deliberate plan, between cock-up and conspiracy, is not easy. Both must be addressed when thinking about what is happening to the NHS and the role Mr Hunt is playing in making it happen. If I have over-emphasised any Machiavellian plan and underestimated his stupidity, I apologise. It is very possible that he did not intend the damage he has done and is doing.

A LONGER GAME

Time, first of all, for a recap. The Lansley Act brought the promise of great riches to private healthcare companies, many of them looking for new outlets for their products beyond the saturated USA market. This was reflected in the triumphalist rhetoric (quoted at the head of this essay) of Mark Britnell – erstwhile director for Commissioning in the NHS and later Global Chairman for Health for gigantic auditing firm KPMG – when the Lansley reforms were first floated. 'In future' he said 'the NHS will be a state insurance provider and not a state deliverer . . . and the NHS will be shown no mercy'. A few years on, the pickings have looked slimmer. Even the low-hanging fruit proved in some cases to have worms at the core. Many private companies, better at winning contracts than delivering care, had discovered that there was less profit to be made than they had anticipated and they were sometimes obliged to treat the contracts won as loss leaders. Aforementioned Circle walked away from Hinchingbrooke hospital when they discovered they could not deliver as they had promised, complaining about the pressure to deal with increasing workloads with no increase in resources. Welcome to the real world of public services.

The obvious conclusion – that the public provision of health services was after all remarkably cost effective and that public bodies were accustomed to dealing with severer 'disciplines' than those of the much-lauded market – was little spoken of in Mr Hunt's office. (A similar story applies to privatisation of social care which is more advanced – 90 per cent being contracted out to privateers – who are squealing about their narrow profit margins. The result – fifteen minute visits to older people with complex problems, staff on slave wages, care homes facing meltdown leaving vulnerable people high and dry, and cash-starved Local Authorities in deficit – makes daily news.) A major player – Bain Capital – who will reappear briefly, but tellingly, at the end of our story, noted that, after strong growth in the first two years of HSCA, contracts going out to the private sector had 'flat lined' with only just under 40 per cent going private in 2015/2016, though the overall numbers continue to increase.

Privateers and their political supporters would therefore have to play a longer game. Rome wouldn't be destroyed in a day, if it had to be dismantled brick by brick under cover of darkness. The challenge would be to undermine the NHS, while somehow keeping the government out of the headlines, except for highly publicised 'more in sorrow than in anger' hand-wringing over clinician's lapses in care and their dereliction of duty, by a Secretary of State no longer responsible for ensuring a comprehensive health service.

Noam Chomsky famously described 'the standard technique of privatisation': 'defund, make sure things don't work, people get angry, you hand it over to private capital'. We could expand this as the strategy of the Ds: Defund, Denigrate, Discredit, Disillusion, Devolve (to destroy Democratic accountability), and finally Dismantle. Thus the path to the fire-sale. Private sector bidders would be able to take over as saviours of a broken health service. Much less would be expected regarding the scope and quality of treatments, care would be delivered by less qualified staff or professionals re-hired at lower salaries, and the profit margins would be more acceptable to shareholders. In the third year of Mr Hunt's tenure, things are looking pretty good for the fire-salesmen.

Firstly, defunding. You could be forgiven for thinking that the NHS has been protected from austerity measures – the policy of punishing the poor for the sins of the very rich – over the last five years. After all, the Coalition agreement 'guaranteed an increase in NHS funding in each year of the parliament'. But, given the source, we might expect this to be a broken promise.

There was a dip in health expenditure in the first two years of the Coalition. This was an historic first: there had been a 3.7 per cent average increase in NHS expenditure year on year since its inception in 1948 until 2010. After the dip, there was a 0.8 per cent annual growth. That might seem generous were it not for the fact, that due to the increase and ageing of the population served, developments in medicine, and government-set targets for increasing staffing levels and the provision of treatments, the demand on the

NHS has risen by 4 per cent per annum. The combination of flatline funding and rising demand means that the service is now losing over 3 per cent of its funding annually and this is set to continue until 2020. The proportion of the Gross Domestic Product spent on healthcare fell by nearly 1 per cent in five years after 2010 to 7.3 per cent – contrasted with 11 per cent for Germany and France. It is due to fall to 6.6 per cent by 2020. We spend 25 per cent less as a percentage of GDP compared with the EU average. (Do we care 25 per cent less for our health and that of our fellow citizens than do our European neighbours?)

Unsurprisingly, hospitals had racked up a £2 billion deficit by the end of 2015 (compared with a surplus of £592 million in 2012–13) and are heading to a financial crash. They have now been instructed to cut staffing levels – 'reduce the head count' is the sinister phrase – and this will ensure that care will deteriorate further. (Staffing shortage was one of the chief causes of the biggest scandal in the NHS in its fifty years, at Mid-Staffs hospital.) There have been directions from the Department of Health to adopt creative accounting proceedings. It has even been suggested that hospitals should look to collaborate with other providers, though as we have seen Lansley's Act has made cooperation (the 'c' word) more difficult. The impact of the defunding strategy has been exacerbated by a 40 per cent reduction in local council budget in five years, with 500,000 less people receiving care and reduced services for most of the rest, and consequently increased pressures on the NHS. More people attend A&E, and patients who are admitted may not be able to be discharged because of lack of social support. Despite this, hospitals have still managed to increase their productivity by nearly 0.5 per cent annually in the last few years – in sharp contrast to the much-lauded private sector.

Statistics like these are often described as 'dry' because it is very difficult when looking at a bar chart to see that it is a portrait of iniquity, of a deception that will cause great suffering. Cameron's claim that health spending is ring-fenced is a whopping mislead but Mr Hunt has handled this masterfully, blaming the growing deficit in the NHS on the service itself, on the staff, on patients who do not use it properly, and on the aforementioned failure of local authorities to provide those services that will prevent patients being trapped in hospital with nowhere to go. Trusts are also blamed for hiring expensive locum agency staff, though a 17 per cent cut in nurse training places had made it inevitable. Underfunding is translated into overspending. Crucially, trusts that have overrun their budgets will be disqualified from taking on future contracts, clearing the path for multinational private providers to mop up.

Shortage of cash is, so Hunt claims, at least in part due to 'waste' estimated at £2 billion (Hunt's favourite number) per year and more recently upped to £5 billion. These figures, though they are very large and very round, even if they were true, are dwarfed by the government-sponsored wastage of resources servicing foolish Private Finance Initiative debts, running competitive tendering and other aspects of marketization of the NHS, and paying for its disruptive interaction with the private sector. This has been estimated at about £10 billion – all squandered for purely ideological reasons. I know I am repeating myself, the result perhaps of being gagged on the pavement by the indifference of passers-by and frustrated by the collusive silence of the mainstream media. (And talking of pavement dialogues, the commonest reason given by passers by for the NHS's financial crisis was 'all those immigrants using our services'. An authoritative study has shown that UK is a net exporter not importer of patients.)

The Chancellor was goaded in Autumn 2015 into emergency funding portrayed as 'a £3.8 billion pounds' cash injection' into the NHS. This was deceptive (of course): most of this sum came from elsewhere in the service, including removal of nursing bursaries (with the predictable result of discouraging entrants and worsening the staffing crisis), and cutting back on the public health budget, hardly the best way to reduce pressures on the NHS. The rest will go into paying off existing £2.2 billion of hospital deficits which will re-accumulate at the same, or a faster, rate.

The 'cash injection' image has also been used to reinforce the impression, beloved of privatisers, that a free-at-the-point-of-need NHS is a 'bottomless pit'. It can never be filled, we are told, not the least because people will abuse services for which they don't pay on the spot (as opposed to through their taxes). The NHS, notwithstanding that it was set up when the country was bankrupt after the War, is therefore 'unsustainable' or 'unaffordable'. This justifies the call for radical reform (i.e. more marketization). The problems will grow as the NHS addresses the impossible task of making £22 billion annual savings by 2020. Rationing is being introduced. Some expensive and effective drugs are no longer available on the NHS. Several CCGs have ruled out funding a variety of surgical procedures of proven benefit. Hearing aids may be provided for only one ear. (Monocles have not yet replaced spectacles.) Patients who smoke or are obese are being denied NHS joint surgery to the outrage and disgust of surgeons who point out that there is no clinical justification for this. Already, waiting lists for elective operations and out-patient appointments have reached the highest levels for a decade, as are waits in Accident and Emergency departments, and to see a GP. General practice has been particularly badly treated with a major reduction in resources and many GPs are reporting that, as the numbers of patients they have to fit into a day is rising, they can no longer practise safely. A&E and maternity departments are closing. The result is that public dis-satisfaction with the NHS jumped between 2015 and 2016 by an unprecedented 8 per cent.

THINGS ARE LOOKING GOOD FOR
THE PRIVATEERS

Denigrate, Discredit, Demoralise: Mr Hunt's Index Finger.

Yes, defunding is starting to deliver. But this has to be handled carefully so that the criticism is directed at the right target. Here Mr Hunt's training in PR has served him well. He has played a blinder in denigrating the NHS and discrediting those who work in it – for the most part individuals whose laces he is not worthy to unloose. Blame is neatly deflected from the government that defunds the service to those who deliver. This, by the way, fits very well with the new duty of the Secretary of State after Lansley: no longer to ensure comprehensive healthcare but merely to 'promote' it.

The instrument Mr Hunt uses for 'promoting' healthcare is his index finger, which knows only one action: wagging. He has been a tireless wagger in his years in office. The blame culture has itself been blamed for the difficulty of righting wrongs where they are evident in the NHS. Even so, Hunt's role as Blamer-in-Chief, is clearly aligned with the long-term strategy of undermining the service. His sanctimonious shock, and his self-portrayal as the defender of the patient against a cruel, careless, incompetent service, has been masterly. Thus the Patients' Champion in a Ministerial Limousine.

The constant sense of Things Going Wrong –

preferably horribly wrong – is useful propaganda for the privateers, not because things don't go wrong in private medicine. They do; but they take place in another country or out of sight in this one. Even so, there is still much work to be done because the vast majority of the population (especially those who owe their lives and limbs to it) still thinks very highly of the NHS. Shockingly, a poll in 2014 showed that the majority of the population would be willing to pay *more* taxes to fund the NHS.

Undermining the standing of professions is an important priority, given that trust in doctors and nurses remains irritatingly high (80–90 per cent) and in politicians very low (less than 20 per cent). So, where there is no particular disaster to exploit, Hunt will make more diffuse attacks on those who work in the NHS, whom he has on more than one occasion described as 'coasting', though they are working at unprecedented levels of intensity. GPs, for example, who now see upwards of seventy patients a day, in addition to all their other duties, have increased their collective annual workload by nearly fifty million appointments per year since 2010.

Hunt is assisted in his work of denigration by journalists who, even when they do not share his ideological hatred of public services and the welfare state, are allergic to denominators which spoil a good scandal by putting blunders in perspective. One crucial denominator – the 1 million people who use the NHS every 36 hours, most of whom are satisfied with the service they receive – is hidden from sight. The absence of denominators enabled the claim that so-called 'never events' (such as operating on the wrong limb) were 'prevalent' in the NHS to be propagated without challenge. The rate of such events is 1:38,000 – three times lower, incidentally, than in US health system.

A reliable way of securing a steady flow of 'scandals' has been the multiplication of inspection regimes. There is no evidence that they promote better overall care. They may sometimes improve measurements on those aspects of care that are prioritised. But the prioritisation of one thing will push everything else back into second place. The Care Quality Commission's (CCQ) expensive, time-consuming inspections of general practice surgeries, have nevertheless been of enormous benefit to Hunt's mission. The CQC is headed by Lord Prior, formerly Chair of the Tory party. He is on record as arguing that the NHS should scrap half of its hospital beds (currently 2.8 per 1,000 people compared with the OECD average of 4.3) and that many hospitals, whom he anticipated would fail his inspection, might then be taken over by US hospital chains, from which much was to be learnt about efficient practice. He cited Circle's spectacular success with Hinchingbrooke – before that lamentable arrangement collapsed. Under Prior's leadership, the CCQ has uncovered shocking statistics such as that some inspected services are below average – a mathematical truism that has power to undermine confidence in the service if they are presented in the right ways to headline writers who can be relied upon to be innumerate.

Major errors and eccentric judgements by the CQC inspectors (often based on nitpicking over 'markers' of safety such as records of curtain cleaning schedules) have been frequent but Prior's outfit is always forgiven by the Department of Health. After all, it is doing its bit to discredit hospitals, general practices, and by extrapolation the entire NHS and the very idea of it. The CQC's eye-popping blunders (for which they have had to apologise) in excoriating some GP surgeries that in fact were of the highest quality add to the overall impression of failure. The Chief Inspector for GPs, Steven Field, described himself in the *Daily Mail* as being ashamed of his profession. This earned Mr Hunt's warm praise for his courage and must surely have done enough to secure him a knighthood.

Mr Hunt seems to have a particular animus against GPs, who deal with 85 per cent of all encounters with patients and may well therefore have their loyalty. The vast majority are skilled, thoughtful individuals who work extremely hard (and harder still as the average number of patients seen per week soars to 350 or more) to get things right in the ten minutes or less allocated to each consultation, and who take on frightening diagnostic responsibilities. No wonder they are alien beings to a failed marmalade salesman. He believes they need to be 'incentivised' either by crude carrots or by whips – echoing his soulmate Oliver Letwin who opined that only if the public sector workers were exposed to private sector 'disciplines' and 'fear' would they raise their game.

The carrot Hunt understands is remuneration. He promised GPs financial incentives to diagnose dementia: £55 a pop to tell someone they are facing a descent into Hell. He offered them bribes to reduce their rate of referral of patients to hospital consultants. At the same time, he threatened to 'name and shame' GPs who do not refer early and often enough patients who might have cancer. It hardly needs pointing out that lowering the threshold for referring people to hospital for expert opinion will mean that more are referred unnecessarily. 'The worried well' will clog up the system, delaying the diagnosis and treatment of those who do have serious disease. This would be irrelevant to those running privatised health services, where the more stuff you sell, the better. Prudent, but appropriate, use of resources doesn't fit into that business model. Getting his whips and carrots in a tangle is understandable for a man who tries to apply marketing models to the provision of medical care in a value-based NHS.

Hunt is perhaps genuinely disorientated by a system such as a publicly funded NHS in which illness is not a market opportunity but a shared social responsibility. And likewise he might be forgiven for thinking that financial incentives are the only way to make doctors more effective and more caring. The desire to do a good job, the motivation to get things right – 'cure some, improve many, comfort all' – and the willingness to shoulder a heavy burden of personal responsibility, do not figure in the world of a PR salesman. So the more generous may think that he is merely confused as to what motivates professionals. Even so, public displays of bribing (and threatening) doctors help to foster the impression that they are morally rather primitive.

Hunt's cunning was particularly in evidence in his use of studies reporting that death rates are higher in patients admitted at weekends than on weekdays. As the authors of the studies repeatedly emphasised, it was not easy to be sure of the reason – or more likely reasons – for the excess mortality. An obvious contributory factor is that weekend admissions tended to be emergencies of more acutely ill patients. Subsequent studies showed the 'weekend effect' to be largely illusory. The headline data provided a political opportunity too good to miss. The Tories had promised a 24/7 NHS in their election manifesto – without specifying any additional resources (though the Department of Health estimated that it would cost just under £1 billion annually and require 11,000 extra staff, none of which was forthcoming. Mr Hunt could now present this as an urgent clinical necessity and moral imperative. If, however, the 24/7 NHS meant increasing *routine* activity at the weekends, this would require either additional funding for more staff or reducing routine activity on weekdays. Financially challenged Trusts had no money to hire extra staff, even if they were available – and this despite a virtual pay freeze for six years. As of 2016, 40 per cent of hospital consultant posts are vacant. Moreover, increasing medical staff would not be enough: nurses, lab staff, radiologists, porters, would all be a vital part of a full 24/7 service. Without an across-the-board increase in staff and resources, Hunt's uncosted, unfunded, and unclear election manifesto promise, which involved removing real protection of junior doctors against dangerously long working hours, would make hospitals less, not more, safe.

Such arguments were easily brushed aside by Spinmeister Hunt in his endless 'more in sorrow than in anger' interviews with gullible media – though the truth did manage to seep through social media and 'Mr Hunt's Lie of the Week' was a very busy blog site. Doctors who pointed out that the NHS was open 24/7 already, not the least for emergencies, but was not yet sufficiently resourced (in particular staffed) to support making Sundays like Wednesdays, were dismissed as dinosaurs resistant to change, as idiots being misled by their union, the British Medical Association, or worse as valuing their social lives above the urgent need to stop unnecessary deaths of their patients.

Ironically, the medical response to a full 24/7 emergency and routine service – not available anywhere else in the world, as Mr Cameron boasted as he launched it as a 2015 election promise – had been positive when it was first floated half a decade ago. There had been much joint work between the medical profession and the Department of Health. Mr Hunt's unilateral imposition on junior doctors of an unsafe and unfair contract (which happened also to discriminate against women doctors) derailed the process. After negotiations broke down, a strike was called by the BMA. It attracted 98 per cent support on a 76 per cent turnout. Mr Hunt, the defender of patients against the self-interested, venal medical profession had to be dragged to mediation, and subsequently he has been tireless in his efforts to head off any solution to the *impasse.* Many outpatient appointments and some elective operations have had to be cancelled. Needless to say his allies in the press spoke of the 'legacy of misery' left by the doctors' strike. One could be forgiven for thinking that Mr Hunt needed this legacy. The privateers most certainly did – and do.

This plan, however, did not deliver the desired result of discrediting the profession: at the time of writing, the public are overwhelmingly in support of the junior doctors. Many remembered, perhaps, being cared for by them. Your essayist and the diehards of Stockport NHS Watch joining the junior doctors' picket on the pavement outside Stepping Hill Hospital do not recall ever being the recipients of so many hoots of support by the passing traffic. This may not last, of course, as a predominantly right-wing press will leap on any adverse event that can be blamed on the strike.

There was, however, one result of Hunt's campaign that was more serious than his failed attempt to discredit NHS staff. The care of ill people, unlike Hotcourses or failing to sell marmalade, really is a matter of life and death. Alarmed by Mr Hunt's self-serving emphasis on how dangerous hospitals were at weekends, some patients postponed presenting themselves or their children until Monday. Patients with strokes and even one or two individuals awaiting transplant, for whom a compatible organ had become available, also held back. This was called 'The Hunt Effect'. Spin has real consequences that cannot be spun away. Mr Hunt's wagging index finger has blood on it.

And demoralising staff likewise looks like translating into equally serious consequences but on a larger scale. Mr Hunt made his promise of 5,000 additional GPs in the NHS even more unrealistic as general practice has been hit by a fall in applications for training, junior hospital doctors are looking to work abroad, and GPs (as well as hospital consultants) are seeking early retirement. As the result of the closure of surgeries, 200,000 patients have been displaced and forced to re-register. 85 per cent of GPs in a 2016 survey thought the profession was in crisis, a Commonwealth Fund Survey found that they were the most stressed GPs in Europe, and 50 per cent felt they could no longer guarantee safe patient care.

In Spring 2016, Mr Hunt launched an investigation into causes of low morale among junior staff. This is analogous to *Salmonella* sponsoring an inquiry into the causes of diarrhoea. One might predict findings that could be summarised in four letters.

PROGRESS REPORT

[Replacing universal NHS provision with a fee-based system] is a good idea in principle but it would be politically suicide for a party that introduced this. They could only really do this if there was a feeling in the country that health services are falling apart.
– Paul Charlson (Vice Chair of Conservative Health), 2013

Defund, denigrate, discredit the service – and demoralise those who work for it. The progress under Mr Hunt's stewardship has been impressive. As *Pulse* magazine described it in February 2016: 'the dominos are falling' with failure in one part of the service accelerating the failure of other parts. The time for wholesale privatisation of the NHS was not ripe when Lansley launched his plan. But now the work of 'ripening the time' is (as I write) well advanced.

And there has been a key development that will assist the denationalisation and privatisation of healthcare: Devolution. Under the guise of increasing the local democratic accountability of health services, responsibility for them has started to be devolved to regions and cities. The first and possibly the biggest devolution – in Greater Manchester – brings together the massive deficit in the hospital finances (nearly £150 million overspend) and the eye-watering shortfall in overall council budgets (estimates vary but all terrifying). The £6 billion made available to the devolved authority falls rather short of the present £10 billion health and social care economy. The gap is to be closed by 'preventing ill health and promoting healthy lifestyles' – in short by a magic wand that will have to be especially powerful, given other social trends, such as a 34 per cent increase in homelessness between 2010 and 2016 and the impact of government policies in increasing poverty and malnutrition – potent causes of illness.

Accelerated defunding apart, devolution will be disastrous, not the least as a result of introducing a new and expensive layer of bureaucracy. Its contribution to enhancing democratic accountability may be judged from the fact that the plan was kept under wraps (hidden even from local MPs) until it was announced just before the 2015 General Election and the 'accountable' officers' deliberations are still hidden from view. However, along with all the other devolutions that are taking place, it will further distance central government from responsibility for the NHS. Indeed, the line of accountability for decisions that are made when the rationing of treatments really starts to bite and the outsourcing of reduced services to the private sector begins, is entirely unclear. The necessary cloak of darkness to hide the dismantling of the NHS, in which it can be sold off in bite-sized chunks, has been created. It will be impossible to find out what, overall, is happening to the healthcare of the nation. And breaking the boundary between means-tested social care and free-at-the-point-of-need health care will disguise the introduction of payment for the latter.

Devolution is the most cunning tool yet for hand-packing the NHS for the convenience of private agglomerations. Another massive reorganisation is chopping the NHS into 44 'footprints' which have 'Sustainability and Transformation Plans' or STPs for short.

Even so, more time will be necessary to complete the auction of our greatest national asset; but Howe's dream is already thirty years old, so patience is in order to cure the populace of what has been described as 'a religious attachment' to the idea of the NHS. Sooner or later blatant deception will no longer be necessary. It is a sign of the confidence of the privateers that the head of a powerful body – with the title of 'NHS Partners Network' – has said that he will make it his first priority to speak to the leaders of STPs about closer working with private healthcare providers. And when, after a pause, the NHS resumes melting like the polar ice cap, there will be little opposition. The idea will have been successfully implanted in the nation's consciousness that the NHS is unaffordable, unsustainable, and dangerous, and was perhaps a bad idea in the first place. The overarching 'D' – deception – will hide the greatest act of destruction in peacetime Britain.

And the fire-sale will begin.

WOULD THIS GET YOU OUT IN THE STREET?

When plunder becomes a way of life for a group of men in society, over the course of time they create for themselves a legal system that authorises it and a moral code that glorifies it.
– Frederic Bastiat

The aftermath of the Second World War saw a moment of political emancipation in Britain. A population, already united in a life and death struggle over five years, maintained the momentum of battle and a sense of social solidarity to establish the Welfare State. For the first time in history, the well-being of the whole population became the explicit concern of the State, through the will of the people.
– Ann Leonard

Of course, the fulfilment of Geoffrey Howe's wicked dream has implications that go beyond the NHS, supremely important though this is. Those of us who passionately support the service, even to the point of shouting in the streets outside a Tory Party conference (and being branded 'ring-nosed crusties' by Boris Johnson) do so for the mixture of reasons that mirror those for which its enemies hate it. It is not for what the NHS does (though hitherto it has done it well, a fact that its enemies have done their best to conceal) but also on account of what it stands for. And if I have spent rather a lot of time on the Character and Motives of a stunning mediocrity such as Mr Hunt, it is because he represents something larger than himself: he is a paradigm case, a small, but potentially lethal, expression of and conduit for destructive trends that are sweeping through Western democracies. He represents a world in which the very idea of commitment to public service is seen as the self-serving rhetoric of individuals protected from the real feedback that comes from customers who can take their business elsewhere. The notion of a job as a vocation, even a 'calling', is deeply suspect as is the idea of a 'covenant' that goes beyond precisely and narrowly defined contractual obligations. The professions – teaching, social work, medicine, nursing – are obliged to redefine themselves, as those whom they care for are re-badged as 'clients' or 'customers' who should be able to define their own needs rather than seeking disinterested guidance. Accountability becomes 'accountantability', the activity of professionals is ever more precisely prescribed, and their contribution defined by what is measurable. The business plan is universal and the professions are businesses like any other. Professionals should henceforth owe their primary loyalty to the firm rather than to professional values or a code of honour, and beyond that to their own wallets. The social contract becomes a nexus of business contracts, competition being the main driver, and monetary and other rewards the sole incentive to excellence.

Although there were worse iniquities in the world outside of my study than the attempted dismantling of the NHS it got me on to the streets in 2012, not only because it was near to hand, closer to my heart, and a cause that seemed as if it might be won, but also because it is a manifestation of something more deeply and widely destructive. Behind the big story of the ideologically-driven vandalisation of the most effective way of delivering life-saving, suffering-reducing, and illness-preventing care, there is a bigger story: deception and corruption in public life; and (evident in many Western democracies) the ever increasing political power of the greedy and the increasing greed of the political classes. The barriers between Big Business and Government, and between corporate interests and political decision making, have all but collapsed. If the Transatlantic Trade and Investment Partnership is agreed, this will be formalised and governments – even those not in thrall to multinationals, financiers, and those who lobby on their behalf – will be impotent to protect public services against predatory private interests. But that is yet another story.

You may think I ought to grow up. Politics and lies, and politicians and pork barrelling, go together like Gin & Tonic. The reason I haven't 'just got over it' is because the selling of the NHS has exposed the extent of our progression in the UK to a banana republic. A shocking proportion of those who shaped the HSCA, who supported its difficult passage through parliament, and of those who voted it onto the statute book, stood to gain personally from the expansion in private healthcare. Over two hundred peers and MPs had their snouts in a trough Lansley's Monster would fill. Parliamentarians and advisers morphed into lobbyists for, and executives of, companies flogging healthcare. Ministers and civil servants glided back and forth through revolving doors connecting public and private sectors. The entire process by which HSCA was imposed on an electorate overwhelmingly opposed to its fundamental aim was effectively a coup.

Neither the privatisation of the NHS, nor the values, principles, and due processes, that have been trampled on in making it possible, have been adequately addressed in the mainstream media – with some honourable exceptions. Most journalists swallowed and regurgitated government press releases. The BBC avoided probing too deeply perhaps for fear of reprisals when the charter renewal has to be approved by government – a government that is considering the idea of replacing the BBC Trust with a body largely populated by political appointees. The failures of Burke's Fourth Estate have contributed to what (to change political philosopher) Karl Marx described as 'false consciousnesses'. It explains why many voted in 2015 for a party that may bring about their financial ruin, or that of their children, if they are foolish enough to fall ill.

The assault on the NHS then is just one manifestation of something that is being replicated throughout our once civil society. In their second term of office, the Tories, unrestrained by the feeble resistance of their Lib-Dem Coalition partners, are even more active in destroying public services, readying them for market. The austerity, imposed by a cabinet that includes several millionaires in addition to Mr Hunt, on an increasingly impoverished underclass makes the first of Chomsky's steps 'Defund' now a universal policy.

One of the justifications of present cruelties is the myth that there are many people who are getting something for nothing. Those who are not in work must be made to work; and those in work must be made to work harder and for less. It was our very own Mr Hunt who proclaimed that Britons ought to learn to work like Chinese. He is not thinking of his friends but the great unwashed who are simply not putting their shoulders to the wheel. And, of course, the Hunt model is taking hold in more and more of the UK. Zero-hours contracts, where employees without any rights can be picked up and put down and who are prevented from complaining about the conditions in which they work or even joining a union for fear of the sack, are symptoms of a wider rot. The unions are facing further major constraints on their ability to take strike action, virtually the only power remaining to workers. Meanwhile, there is a plan – only temporarily stalled due to House of Lords opposition – drastically to reduce the in-work benefits of those whose hard labour does not attract a living wage.

In short, the war against the poor (in 2016 this constituted 16 per cent of the UK population) and their unnecessary and undesirable children – excused by tenth-rate economics but motivated by first-water vindictiveness – is now well under way as their benefits and the fabric of public services on which they depend is being ripped up by thugs who are constantly telling us how much they care. The number of children in absolute poverty is set to reach 2.6 million and the homeless total 1 million by 2020. Rough sleepers have doubled in six years. Life is being made unbearable Hell for those at the bottom of the pile – people with disabilities, their carers, hardworking individuals who are exploited with low wages, their children – in this, one of the world's richest economies, to fulfil the punitive dreams of the free market fundamentalists. The mantra of needing to live within our means and to pay down the national debt has long been exposed, by many respected economists, as an ideological choice rather than an economic necessity. Many suffer appalling hardship so that a minority, who already have more than they could consume or enjoy, might prosper.

The tenacity, patience, and attention to detail with which the life chances of the precariat are being unpicked would have been admirable had it not been devoted to such a wicked cause. Ours is an 'undeveloping' nation, in which all services – from Sure Start for the very young to Employment support for the disabled, to home care for the very old and frail – are being decimated.

The attack on benefits, housing and healthcare is bearing evil, if entirely predictable, fruit. The ultimate expression of the assault on the most vulnerable is the increase in death rates seen in 2015 – the biggest since the 1960s and the third increase in successive years. The 27,000 excess deaths – an appalling harvest of sorrow – are presumably a price worth paying for defending the interests of one's friends and placing the insatiable greed of the affluent above the basic needs of the less well off.

The Dirty War against the poor is assisted by the increased use of statutory instruments that do not have to be debated in parliament and, with an opposition in disarray, can be implemented without notice. These empower governments to disempower those they govern, whether it is to remove or diminish benefits or to disenfranchise a million of those voters most likely to be damaged by them. As the work of hollowing out democracy continues – the anti-sleaze rules against dishing out top and plum government jobs to friends, introduced in 1990s, are being relaxed – Government and Big Business have rolled out the red carpet for a succession of visiting tyrants, signing high-profile business deals that bring photo-opportunities for ministers and economic opportunities for those whose interests they share.

Earlier, I mentioned one of the arguments advanced for replacing the NHS by an insurance-based service; namely that the costs of the present arrangements are not appreciated by those who use the service. If people don't pay for things, we are told, they won't appreciate them and will be inclined to abuse them. Of course, the vast majority of people who use the NHS *have* paid for it out of their taxes: 'free at the point of use' does not mean free. Except that, for some very rich individuals, it does mean free. The Panama Papers and other leaks of information have given us an insight into how the rich puppet masters of those who govern us avoid their fiscal duties. The loss of tax revenue from the kind of aggressive tax avoidance schemes that Mr Hunt has used and the offshore tax havens (some actively protected by the Government against EU legislation) used by many senior Tories and corporations, and the repatriation of profits to low tax jurisdictions, amounts to many tens of billions. This is enough and more to close the black hole in NHS finances. The latest estimate of £34 billion annual unpaid tax is almost exactly the sum necessary to raise NHS funding to the European average.

A ten-year-old child can see that multinational free-riders parasitize the civilisation built out of other people's taxes. If others were able to match their 'tax-efficient' regimes, we would have no hospitals, street lights, police force, army, schools – I hardly need go on.

The focus, however, has been on 'benefit scroungers' whose cost to the nation is a minute percentage of that of millionaire scroungers who, enjoying the civilisation funded by other people's taxes, walk the corridors of power and have the ear of government. The vicious and vindictive bedroom tax imposed on severely disabled individuals and their carers provides an instructive contrast. Tax men hunt down a person in a wheel chair living near the breadline but seem relaxed about the super-rich super-yachting round the world.

The banking class that brought us close to irreversible ruin less than a decade ago now enjoys increasing access to the Chancellor and the case for 'light touch' regulation that took us to the edge of the abyss from which we were rescued by the much-derided Labour government is growing stronger by the day. The consequence in a society in which the richest 1 per cent of the population now have as much wealth as the poorest 57 per cent will be further polarisation. The rich will get richer not by making anything anyone can use – not even Hotcourses, listings agencies or PR firms – but out of making money move around the monetary system. Their wealth will make the world more expensive and life more impoverished for the rest of us, though, like Mark Zuckerberg of Facebook, they will flaunt their generosity to charities. Ostentatious philanthropy is much more enjoyable than paying fair taxes that will support truly good causes like the NHS.

'We are all in it together' is the mantra of the PR

man occupying 10 Downing Street. And in a sense he is right. We are all aboard the Good Ship UK. But some are sipping champagne at the captain's table while increasing numbers of others are below decks drinking bilge water. Meanwhile, Cameron tells the world that his is the party of the working class and the poor; and he is cheered for this by the Conservative faithful who must relish such hypocrisy. We now know to insert the word 'not' before each of his claims. When challenged on his commitment to the NHS, Cameron wept tears for his dead son Ivan who had been cared for in the NHS. I am sure that his tears were sincere, but they are the forerunners of many tears to come, rolling down the cheeks of the others for their sick children – when the first person they meet in an hour of mortal danger will be an accountant who tells them that they cannot afford the care they need in that hour.

England is increasingly an ex-democracy, where power lies with unelected money men and the lobbyists and with the media who speak for them. Even so, it would not only be defeatist but irresponsible to conclude that defending the NHS against predators is a lost cause. For the foreseeable future, your radicalised essayist (who was a signatory in 2010 to a letter to the *Guardian* urging everyone to vote Liberal Democrat – how far he has travelled!) will continue shouting slogans in the streets, writing and distributing leaflets, filling envelopes, knocking on doors, and generally being a pest. He will campaign for reinstatement of

the founding principles of the NHS as a publicly funded, publicly provided service, free at the point of need.
Success seems unlikely because those who support the
NHS lack the patronage of the parliamentary representatives of Virgin, Circle, Serco, Capital, KPMG and
their like. If, therefore, in due course, there is no NHS,
I will not be surprised. If I am proved wrong, no-one
will be happier (or more surprised) than I.

CODA

The New Year's Honours List in 2016 was generous
to those who assisted the realisation of Lord Howe's
wicked dream. Lynton Crosby, the Tory's campaign
manager for the 2015 General Election, was imported
from Australia to exercise his skills in ensuring that
the national debate was re-directed away to distracting
trivia, and messages were distorted, such that many
voted against their own interests. He is now *Sir* Lynton
Crosby. Andrew Lansley, whom all parties are agreed
has inflicted more damage on the NHS than any of
his predecessors as Secretary of State for Health – has
been ennobled. As 'Lord Lansley of Cambridge' he has
joined Bain, a private equity firm, advising them on
how to increase their share of our greatest national asset. If only Lansley had been given whatever he wanted
– ermine or millions – a decade ago, who knows how
much waste, and possibly how many lives might have

been saved. Things to savour when you are waiting in unrelieved pain in ever-lengthening queues, when the NHS has become a distant memory, the welfare state has been trashed, and first-class public services have become a thing of the past.

Cry, beloved country.

5

– 'All Is Number': Mathematics, Reality and the Madness of Max Tegmark –

For over a decade I have been working on a Big Book on the nature of time: *Of Time and Lamentation: Reflections on Transience.* Anyone who thinks about time has, sooner or later, to engage with physics and, more particularly, to rescue time from its jaws. In the Long March to the much-trumpeted and long-awaited Theory of Everything, natural science has done some terrible things to time.

The story begins with the Scientific Revolution in the 16th and 17th centuries, and giants such as Galileo, Kepler and Newton. The science of mechanics that connected the earth and heavens through laws encompassing the great movements of the planets through space and the small movements of the objects dropped on the floor reduced time to a dimension. Time became a member of a quartet along with the three dimensions of space. The habit in mechanics of representing time as a kind of space came to affect all of natural science. This set the scene for the ultimate merging of space and time in space-time.

The merger was announced by Hermann

Minkowski in 1907, two years after the Special Theory of Relativity had been published by his erstwhile pupil Albert Einstein:

Henceforth, space by itself, and time by itself, are doomed to fade away into mere shadows, and only a kind of union will preserve an independent reality.

The replacement of space and time by space-time is presented as a triumph of scientific understanding, though the use of the stand alone temporal term 'henceforth' at the beginning of Minkowski's proclamation might have raised the eyebrows of the un-bewitched.

Denying the separate identity of time and space – for example the temporal interval between the beginning and end of your reading Minkowski's sentence and the spatial gap between the words set out on the page – was just the start. Next to go was tensed time (past, present, and future). This was followed by definite intervals and locations of time. 'When' and 'how long' were seen to have no objective reality. Time was shrivelled to 'little t' that had no characteristics other than magnitudes whose size depended on the frame of reference from which they were measured.

Worse was to come. In quantum mechanics, the very notion of a time interval between events is problematic. Carlo Rovelli, among others, speculated that time might disappear altogether when quantum mechanics and general relativity are united in the Theory of Everything.

In their monumental *The Singular Universe and the Reality of Time*, Roberto Unger and Lee Smolin have argued that the failure of contemporary physics to find a place for time as we know it, far from being a triumph, is an intellectual disaster. They blame this on the central role of mathematics in physical science. And I am inclined to agree. There is no place in the mathematical world picture for 'now', 'later' and other fundamental aspects of time; for time as it is lived, the time of our lives, time as you and I experience it. None of this would matter philosophically or existentially were it not for the fact that natural science is thought to be the last word on what is really real. If you want to know the time, ask a policeman, runs the old song. But if you want to know what time is, ask a physicist, runs the new orthodoxy. And alas and alack, time according to physicists, if it is allowed to exist at all, is a poor shrivelled thing, a pure quantity, something that is so lacking in character as to allow itself to be placed under space (designated by 's') as a denominator (s/t = speed), or multiplied by itself (t^2) in descriptions of accelerated motion) or by the strange character i (the square root of minus 1) in equations linking it with space. No-one would have thought of doing any of those things to a piece of lived time such as a sunny afternoon or a Bargain Break Weekend in Bruges.

PHYSICS, MATHEMATICS AND REALITY

My decade-long investigation into time kept on raising problems that were not in the original prospectus.
This is the way with philosophical inquiries: if they are
conducted at the right depth, they find themselves en-
tering other areas of inquiry. Time led me to memory,
anticipation, the structures of consciousness, even to
the question of free will. But, as will be evident from
the story so far, the most important digression was
into the relationship between mathematics and reality. What should we make of the dominance of mathematical physics in our thinking about the fundamental
nature of the world?

The ultimate authority of natural science is not
something that is preached only by physicists and
science groupies to the innocent and gullible masses
for whom metaphysics does not rank as highly as being in on the gossip, making a living, or dreaming
of fame. Quite a few professional philosophers have
decided that the inquiry into traditional concerns of
metaphysics – space, time, causation, what kind of
stuff makes up the world – should be led by physicists. The eminent philosopher Hilary Putnam was
speaking for increasing numbers of his colleagues
when he said:

I do not believe that there are any longer any philosophical
problems about Time; there is only the physical problem of

determining the exact physical geometry of the four-dimensional continuum that we inhabit.

The metaphysician James Ladyman has more recently declared that he wears the charge of 'scientism' as a badge of honour. The role of the philosopher, it seems, is that of a humble assistant, perhaps helping to find ways in which different theories across the sciences can be unified or at least rationally connected.

There are many reasons for resisting this claim but the most important is that natural science marginalises the human world. Physics cannot accommodate much of what fills our lives. Worse, it seems remote from the physical world as we experience it in everyday life. Not only is the world reduced to a physical world empty of humanity but also (as the critic of philosophical scientism Susan Stebbing put it) the physical world is confused with the world according to physics. I have already deplored what physics does to time (and come to that space, which is, among other things fused with time). Worse still, it treats matter – the stuff of cups and saucers, and roads, and trees and soil – even more badly. Under the gaze of classical physics, seemingly static and coherent objects break up into swarms of restless atoms. And quantum mechanics seems to take away the individual identity of even these components. Quantum field theory and quantum entanglement apparently demonstrate that the physical world is not composed of discrete, independent, localised objects.

It was concerns such as these that gatecrashed *Of Time and Lamentation*. And they bring me to the theme of this essay, though I first want to say a couple of things about physics.

The first is that (it should go without saying) it is spectacularly successful, generating powerful theories of huge scope that connect the most disparate phenomena, making predictions of staggering precision, and providing the theoretical underpinning for the ubiquitous and diverse technologies that support us in every moment of our lives. Thanks to applied physics, we have life expectancies, health expectancies, comfort expectancies and fun expectancies unimaginable to our pre-scientific forebears. And this practical applicability extends to theories that deal in arcana such as positrons and their subatomic kin that began life as the predicted progeny of the most rarefied mathematical interpretations of the most esoteric observations. Physics has played a key role in creating a world in which work and social interaction and even to some extent our sense of who we are, is decisively shaped by the electronic devices made possible by quantum theory. This awe-inspiring theoretical and practical power and precision seems to justify the view expressed by Hilary Putnam that 'scientific realism is the only philosophy of science that does not make the success of science a miracle'. Things out there must in some important sense correspond to the way they are portrayed in physics.

The second thing is the extent to which mathematics has, as the physicist Eugene Wigner has pointed out in a justly famous paper ('The Unreasonable Effectiveness of Mathematics in the Natural Sciences'), played 'a sovereign role', in guiding the endeavour of physics to arrive at the most general account of the physical world. As R. W. Hamming expressed it (in 'The Unreasonable Effectiveness of Mathematics') 'The mathematical formulation of the physicist's often crude experience leads in an uncanny number of cases to an amazingly accurate description of a large class of phenomena' ˉ suggesting that mathematical language touches on deeper truths than are accessible to our senses.

If we combine the belief that physics is telling us what the universe at the fundamental level really is with the observation that mathematics lies at the heart of physics, we may conclude that our universe is intrinsically mathematical. This claim has many famous adherents. I referred in the opening essay to Galileo's assertion that 'the book of nature is written in the language of mathematics'. This certainly determined the future direction of the natural sciences, placing quantities, measurements, and the laws derived from measurements at the heart of its practice. The faith that nature was at bottom a system of magnitudes has been richly rewarding, guiding the discovery of laws of increasing generality and predictive and explanatory power, that connect ever more disparate areas of inquiry promising an ultimate (mathematical) Theory of Everything. The scientist Mary Somerville noted how 'The progress of modern science, especially within the last five years, has been remarkable for a tendency to simplify the laws of nature, and to unite detached branches by general principles.' She was writing in 1834.

Wigner cites a couple of remarkable examples of how Galilean faith in an essentially numerate Nature was rewarded. His first example is especially striking: Newton's law of gravitation. Newton noted a numerical coincidence between the speed of falling bodies on earth, the curved pathways taken by thrown rocks, and the elliptical orbit of planets. He arrived, by an extraordinary leap of imagination, at a relatively simple mathematical law with a universal applicability. 'The law of gravity which Newton reluctantly established and which he could verify to an accuracy of about 4 per cent has proved to be accurate to less than a ten thousandth of a per cent.' Less than 0.0001 per cent! This illustrates Hamming's more general point that

science is composed of laws which were based on a small, carefully selected set of observations, often not measured very accurately originally; but the laws have later been found to apply over much wider ranges of observation and much more accurately than the original data justified. Not always . . . *but often enough to require explanation.* [Italics mine.]

An even more astonishing example, invoked by Wigner was the importation of a highly abstract form of mathematics, namely matrix algebra, into quantum mechanics. This has proved spectacularly effective in helping scientists to understand and predict what is going on at the subatomic level. Matrix algebra was originally invoked in response to the observation that some rules of computation given by physicist Werner Heisenberg (of the famous Uncertainty Principle) were formally identical with the rules of computation with matrices established in the 19th century. Application of the rules of matrix mechanics to situations in which Heisenberg's rules did not apply (indeed were meaningless) made predictions that agreed with experimental data to – wait for it – within one part in 10,000,000.

The great theories of recent physics have been mathematics-led, and by physicists with a pronounced sense of mathematical beauty, though they have been triggered by, and exposed to testing against, observations. It is this that has made respectable 2,500-year-old ideas that might in an earlier century have been dismissed as mysticism. I am talking about the semi-mystical belief, ascribed by Aristotle to the pre-Socratic philosopher Pythagoras, that 'All Is Number'. Not only are 'the principles of mathematics . . . the principles of all things' (as Aristotle put it) but the very fabric of the universe is made of numbers. In fact, a careful reading of the patchy textual record absolves Pythagoras of being a full-blown Pythagorean. As Leonid Zhmud says, 'we can attribute to Pythagoras only the idea of similarity and correspondence of some notions with numbers' ('"All is Number"? "The Basic doctrine" of Pythagoreanism reconsidered').

MATHEMATICS AND REALITY

It is important to distinguish different ways of conceiving the relationship between mathematics and the material world. There are still some who insist that mathematics is simply a useful tool; the most effective tool for gathering up data that are themselves intrinsically numerical, for generalising them, and for identifying patterns in them. Mathematics, they argue, is just a notational system and the laws that correspond to the patterns are to a greater or lesser degree conventional, essentially mind-portable, simplifications of what is out there. What is envisaged is a natural world that is ordered mathematically but is not itself made of mathematical stuff. Mathematics is the *language* of the book of nature – in which we may communicate with it – but not nature itself. This may shade into the bolder idea that mathematics provides us not only with the most convenient but also with the most faithful and comprehensive account of what is 'out there'.

The next step commands less widespread assent: according an independent existence to 'mathematical objects'. Numbers, geometrical figures, and more exotic mathematical entities such as complex and imaginary numbers have a stand alone reality. Ascribing reality to such objects is called Platonism, after the philosopher for whom abstractions accessed through the intellect were real; indeed, he claimed they were more real than the transient objects evident to our senses. Full-scale Platonism places these items on a pedestal: they belong in Heaven, or Eternity, as unchanging pure and perfect beings. Few contemporary Platonists subscribe to all of these ideas but they remain fascinated by the beautiful internal logic of numbers – which seems to be discovered rather than invented – and by the way mathematical techniques – ideas invented for the fun of it – turn out to be just what is needed to make sense of the physical world. They are found to provide the solution to physical problems that had not even been conceived at the time the mathematics was invented. A much-cited example is non-Euclidean geometry and tensor calculus that turned out to be the key to formulating the General Theory of Relativity many years after their inventors had died.

And so we reach industrial strength Pythagoreanism, one of whose most flamboyant and prominent exponents is the theoretical physicist 'Mad' (an epithet in which he rejoices) Max Tegmark. According to his 'mathematical universe hypothesis' (MUH), natural realities are mathematical structures – a set of abstract entities with relations between them. This is to be understood literally. Consider for example the bright stuff that enables you to see the page you are currently reading. According to Tegmark (in his *Our Mathematical Universe: My Quest for the Ultimate Nature of Reality*),

[Light] is simply a wave rippling through the electromagnetic field, so if our physical world is a mathematical structure, then all the light in our Universe (which feels quite physical) corresponds to six numbers at each point in space-time (which feels quite mathematical).

Light boils down to numbers at space-time points that are in turn identical with the numbers that define them.

The world according to Tegmark is a nexus of pure magnitudes that are not the magnitude of anything; more a structure abstracted from patterns of magnitudes. He proposes not only that all reality is mathematical but – combining Platonism with his Pythagoreanism – also that *only* the mathematical is real. What he calls his 'mathematical monism' denies that anything exists other than mathematical objects: 'our physical world is not only *described* by mathematics but . . . is mathematics'. Even conscious experience is composed of mathematical substructures that are mysteriously (but very conveniently) 'self-aware'. This last claim may be difficult to swallow but at least it deals with Putnam's witty critique of Platonism 'that it seems flatteringly incompatible with the fact that we think with our brains, not with immaterial souls'. The incompatibility vanishes if our brains are made of Platonic mathematical objects.

Tegmark's hypothesis does not make clear which mathematical objects we should include in his universe. They are, after all, a rather mixed bunch encompassing homely items such as the cardinal numbers (1, 2, 3 etc.) and triangles, more exotic ones such as complex numbers (like the square root of minus 1, sets, and matrices) and more active ones such as equations and wave functions. But there is a deeper problem with Tegmark's Platonic paradise. It is frozen. Why? Because 'the only intrinsic properties of a mathematical structure are its relations, timeless and unchanging'. Change is an illusion and so, also, is time.

Naturally, we might be puzzled why he wrote his book. Was it not because he believed that he might change our views as a result of our reading it – in relation to which there is a 'before' and 'after'? Surely he does not believe that the changes in our views (and his part in changing them) are not ultimately real? It is clear that something has gone horribly wrong as a result of taking to the limit the notion that the ultimate reality of the physical world is something that can only be expressed mathematically.

Before we address this, it is worth noting the irony – flagged up by the American philosopher Willard van Orman Quine – that physics, which began as the most hard-headed of the sciences, should have, in its theoretical upper reaches, made the world evaporate to abstractions:

Physical objects . . . evaporated into space-time regions; but this was the outcome of physics itself. Finally, the regions went over into pure sets; still, the set theory itself was there for no other reasons than the need for mathematics as an adjunct to physical theory.
– 'Whither Physical Objects?'

REALITY BEYOND MATHEMATICS

How did we get to a picture of nature as a frozen, windless, oasis-less desert of mathematical entities and structures? The first and most important reason is that we exaggerate the 'unreasonable effectiveness' of mathematics. Wigner makes this clear in his arti-cle: the effectiveness of mathematics is something of a 'put up job' where a mathematized universe matches a universalised mathematics. He points out the things that are not included in physics. 'The laws of nature,' he says, 'are all conditional statements and they re-late only to a very small part of our knowledge of the [physical] world'. Even in classical mechanics – which is 'the best known prototype of a physical theory' – Newton's famous laws tell us very little about what actually happens. They have nothing to say about 'the existence, the present positions, and velocities of bodies'. To solve the equations of motion, we need not only the mathematical laws but also the initial or starting conditions and the boundaries within which a necessarily closed system operates. The laws predict how the material of the universe behaves only in a given scenario but do not specify the scenario. In short, they lack within themselves anything to operate on or within. Supplementing the number of laws or discovering laws of greater generality would not dispense with the need to have initial conditions – which is why the attempts by physics to trespass on the territory of theologians and produce their own creation story have proved so unconvincing. You cannot simultaneously generate the laws of nature *and* the stuff upon which they operate; or create the latter out of the former.

Wigner acknowledges that the mathematical account of the world not only fails to encompass its experienced, phenomenal qualities (of which more presently) but also the singularity of actual physical events that really take place, at a particular location in space and time. Mathematical physics by itself predicts only general possibilities defined by co-variance of patterns of quantities, not the actual events that take place in actual places. The absence of singularity (leaving aside the contested singularity at the start of the universe) in the laws of physics, indeed the absence of actuality, uncovers the true nature of what mathematics reveals of reality: only its most general form, pattern, or structure but not the content or stuff of reality itself. Our quantitative equations can, with dazzling success, predict certain quantitative aspects of events but they do not encompass all aspects even of those events they predict. They do not take us down to actuality – actualities which necessarily occur and are experienced in particular localities.

So we can accept and be grateful for the 'unreasonable' effectiveness of mathematics without at the same time feeling obliged to believe that the universe is in some sense intrinsically mathematical or that mathematics is the most faithful portrait of the world. We investigate the world mathematically in order to overcome the fact that, individually and collectively, we approach it from a particular place or angle. It is our way of getting outside of our perspective or location, though it is only from a particular perspective or location that experience is possible and only in such locations do particular events occur. Mathematics is thus a bridge between what we are and what is 'out there', without being constitutive either of what we are or of the physical world. It is a lens turning our shared experience into an image of a world that vastly outsizes both ourselves and the parishes in which we each live.

And it is, of course, obvious – to return to Wigner – that for most of the history of physics, the most mathematized account of the natural world still has a non-mathematical residue. The laws of physics do not have the mathematical purity of axioms or proofs. Consider, for example, Newton's Second Law of Motion we all learned at school $f = ma$: the acceleration of a body will be proportional to the force applied to it. Neither 'acceleration' nor 'force' is a purely mathematical concept or object, in the way that the number 2 is. The differences between the components – between f and m and a – is not the same as the differences between two mathematical entities. That a law such as $f = ma$ is not like 2 + 2 = 4 is highlighted by the fact that 2 + 2 = 4 is necessary, true in all possible worlds, while the law is contingent. That is why that 2 + 2 = 4 is hardly a discovery comparable to Newton's Second Law. And when we do have pure numbers – as in the case of dimensionless physical constants – they are brute facts, a limit to explanation and intelligibility.

Roberto Unger and Lee Smolin have argued (in *The Singular Universe and the Reality of Time*) that the 'unreasonable' power of mathematics in the natural sciences that Wigner spoke of is in fact entirely reasonable because it picks its targets with care, leaving out mathematically intractable phenomenal qualities (the things we experience such as colours and sounds), time, and of course everything connected with value and significance. It confines itself to those aspects of reality which it is particularly suited to capture, reflect, or express. Mathematics

is an understanding of nature emptying the world of all particularity and temporality: that is a view of the world without either individual phenomena or time.

As pioneer of quantum mechanics and computers, John von Neumann put it:

[A] mathematical formulation that is chosen to represent the underlying problem may represent it only with certain idealizations, simplifications . . . .This . . . is closely related to the methodological observation that a mathematical formulation necessarily represents only a (more or less) explicit theory of some phases (or aspect) of reality not reality itself.

The kinds of things that mathematical physics gets staggeringly right are precisely the things that you would expect it to get right. It might predict with amazing accuracy the quantity, location and wavelength of such and such nanometres of light but not the experience of red. Likewise, a GPS device can guide us from one place defined as a mathematical point in space to another also defined as a mathematical point in space with a degree of precision that would not have been possible had not General Relativity been valid; but it says nothing about either place or about the places between them. What it is like to go from A to B, what it is like being at A or B, and what A or B are like (beyond being a group of numbers in a system of coordinates) are realities beyond the reach of mathematics.

We should bear this in mind when an appropriate respect for the quantitative achievements of science seduces us into an uncritical acceptance of all its demands to alter our understanding of the nature of reality in the way that Carlo Rovelli has described so vividly (in *Seven Brief Lessons on Physics*):

Within Einstein's equation there is a teeming universe, a phantasmagorical succession of predictions that resemble the delirious ravings of a madman, but which have all turned out to be true . . . The theory describes a colourful amazing world where universes explode, spaces collapse into bottomless holes, time sags and slows near a planet, and the unbounded extensions of interstellar space ripple and sway like the surface of the sea.

Only up to a point, Signor Rovelli. We exaggerate the power of mathematics, Unger and Smolin argue, because we overlook its selective realism:

The less we grasp the non-mathematical reasons for the [restricted] application of mathematics (and . . . we understand them only very incompletely), the more enigmatic and disconcerting the application of mathematics will appear to be. We will be tempted to bow down to mathematics as the custodian of nature's secrets.

Quantitative science at its most fundamental presents nature denatured. As Unger and Smolin note acidly:

The self-denying ordinance that is the source of [mathematics'] power provides no license to impose that ordinance on the whole of experience. Scientism is not science.

NOR IS SCIENTISM WARRANTED BY SCIENCE

The two fundamental and ubiquitous aspects of reality missing from the mathematical portrait of the universe are time and the *experience* of reality. As for the latter, the exsanguinated universe of physics is illustrated in the example given by Mad Max Tegmark cited earlier: light. You may recall that for Tegmark, 'all the light in our Universe (which feels quite physical) corresponds to six numbers at each point in space-time (which feels quite mathematical)'. Light as pure mathematics! I think not. Seeing is not counting; sunbathing is not number-bathing. But this is where the privileging of quantities over qualities – implicit in Galileo's assertion already referred to that 'the book of nature is written in the language of mathematics' – may lead to if taken as the literal and entire truth of nature.

Galileo's distinction between primary and secondary qualities is an early warning. (See 'Humanity: Neither God's Work nor a Piece of Nature'). Primary qualities are size, shape, and number which, Galileo argues, are intrinsic properties of the natural world because it is impossible to imagine physical objects lacking them. Secondary qualities – such as colours, smells and sounds – which are dependent for their existence on conscious minds have no place in the natural world seen clearly. As historian of science Bernard Cohen has pointed out, the emphasis on mechanics supported this view. Motion is central to the idea of nature developed in physical science – as is captured in the precept that 'to be ignorant of motion is to be ignorant of nature'. The essence of motion is number, the essence of nature is motion, and consequently the essence of nature is number.

The special status accorded to the quantitative over the qualitative is reinforced by the centrality of measurement in science and in the technology which rightly astonishes us and to which we owe so much. 'Measure began our might,' as W. B. Yeats said. Measurements seem to be cognitively superior to direct experiences because they are repeatable and we can safely agree or fruitfully disagree on them. Their repeatability, such that if we all do the measurement correctly we shall report the same result, is a testament to their objectivity and hence to their being true of objects that go beyond our immediate experiences. Direct sense experiences will vary from moment to moment, from person to person, which brands them as unreliable and hence not quite real. We cannot experience each other's experiences and we will often differ over them – what something looks like, how much time has passed, and so on – but we can share measurements. We may disagree as to how long a journey is if we rely on our experiences rather than a pedometer.

The repeatability of measurement, and the way the measured world coheres, does not, of course, justify the conclusion that all that is real is measurable. Even less does it imply that reality is essentially numerical.

Not even measurements are pure numbers for the obvious reason that they are expressed in units which are more than numbers. 'Six inches' is not pure '6'. The act of measurement, what is more, involves countless sensory experiences, even when what is measured is highly abstract. Think of all the sensory experiences of the physicists journeying to CERN in Switzerland to contribute to the hunt for the Higgs' boson. Only by overlooking this can we imagine that we leave our senses behind when we make a measurement, notwithstanding that the sense experiences are irrelevant to the datum that is obtained – the number on the dial, the dots on the screen. Because this is forgotten, we can be deluded into thinking that a world drained of phenomenal reality is the world seen as it really is.

The marginalisation of all that we actually experience, never mind the pain, pleasure, and significance of things (mere 'tertiary qualities', as we discussed in the opening essay) in favour of the reality of the ruler, the clock, and the weighing machine, that began in the 17th century, lies at the start of the journey that ultimately led to a vision of the world as mathematical structures. The realm revealed to everyday experience is meanwhile discredited as a distorted or cloudy image of a reality, hidden from our gaze until its mathematical structure is unveiled by mathematical modelling on the basis of the findings of quantitative experimental science.

Mathematical science gets nimbler as it sheds

baggage; but the baggage it sheds is the world we live in, which underpins the 'there' of what is there. The *thisness* and *whatness and for-me-ness and for-you-ness and here-and-nowness* are discarded as mere Ness monsters inhabiting the world of naïve consciousness. We are left with a Pythagoreanism of numbers in space-time, with the latter becoming an insubstantial mist of numbers.

Many scientists are, of course, aware of this deficiency of purely quantitative science, and are not entirely happy about it. Among them is one of the greatest physicists of the 20th century, Richard Feynman. In a lecture towards the end of his life, he noted that:

Today we cannot see whether Schrodinger's equation contains frogs, musical composers, or morality – or whether it does not.

Schrodinger's Wave Equation is the fundamental equation of the most powerful set of theories in all of science – quantum theory. Less perceptively, he anticipated:

the next great awakening of human intellect may well produce a method of understanding the qualitative content of equations.

The notion that (secondary) qualities might be rescued by a new qualitative understanding of (mathematical) equations is probably self-contradictory but the acknowledgement of what is missing from the mathematical portrait of the world is welcome – particularly from such an elevated source.

(MATHEMATICAL) PHYSICS IN TROUBLE

And this kind of fundamental self-questioning may be just what physics itself needs. There has been increasing restlessness among some physicists that mathematics-led physics has in places finally parted company even from the highly processed measurements used in advanced science. The mathematics that takes us beyond experience eventually loses touch with the possibility of crucial observations that may confirm the superiority of one theory to its rivals. In a much-discussed recent paper in the leading science journal *Nature* ('The Scientific Method. Defend the Integrity of Physics') the authors – George Ellis, an eminent mathematician and Joe Silk, a leading physicist – have protested against the recent abandonment of empirical testability (and possible falsification) as a criterion of a truly scientific theory. Their targets are philosophers of science such as Sean Carroll and Richard Dawid who have argued that if a theory is sufficiently elegant and seems to have explanatory power, it need not be tested or testable experimentally. Carroll and Dawid were responding to the criticism that certain theories – of the inflationary origin of the cosmos, string theory,

and the increasingly popular multiverse hypotheses –
are compatible with almost any observational result.
Far from belonging to the much-touted 'Theory of
Everything' where quantum mechanics and General
Relativity are united, they are examples of what Paul
Steinhardt has with delicious scorn dubbed 'Theories
of Anything'. String theory, for example, would need a
particle accelerator bigger than the universe to test it.
As for the multiverse hypothesis, and the suggestion
that the so-called 'cold spot' in cosmic background ra-
diation is a signature of something outside of our universe resulting from quantum entanglement, it strikes
many as beyond tenuous. The notion that there is an
infinity of universes prompts Ellis and Silk to quote the
great mathematician David Hilbert who pointed out
that 'while infinity is needed to complete mathematics, it exists nowhere in nature'. Equally vulnerable is
the idea that the universe has ten dimensions of space,
seven of which are rolled up very small or (boldest/
wildest of all) that the universe is a single wave function, a landscape described by 10^{512} string theories.

Such theories are the end point of the ascent of
physics to pure mathematics. The pursuit of the Grand
Universal Theory or GUT seems to have led it to a
place where it disappears up its own . . . well I leave
you to complete the sentence.

REALITY ELUDES MATHEMATICS

The other consequence of seeing the universe as a mathematical structure is that, since structures are stable, static, indeed frozen, change is not possible. Which brings me back to the point where my foray into the relationship between mathematics and reality started: the terrible things physics does to time, firstly reducing it to a mere parameter, next stripping it of tenses, then denying it the capacity to have even quantitative values separate from space, and finally disappearing altogether. As Unger and Smolin point out, a world of eternal structures has no history and this is particularly awkward given that cosmology is always dealing in Grand Narratives. There is, after all, supposed to be a sequence of events. The Big Bang that started it all off occurred at a definite time (13.8 billion years ago). It was followed by the succession of changes that resulted in: the galaxies; the emergence of life on at least one planet; the evolution of life towards higher forms; and eventually conscious life, one advanced form of which was physicists who have become aware of one version of this history.

We don't have to think of anything as grand as the history of the universe to find something that lies beyond the grasp of mathematics. The pre-Socratic Greek philosopher Zeno thought he had showed that something as simple as running was impossible because mathematics could not grasp it. Consider my hurrying to catch a bus waiting for me. The driver's kindness would be ill-rewarded if reality were purely mathematical. In order to reach the bus, I have to halve the distance separating me from it; and then I will have to cover the first half of the remaining half; and then the first quarter of the remaining quarter. You can see where this is going: *ad infinitum* not to the 99 bus. It would appear that I must complete an infinite number of mathematical steps in order to board the bus. Things are even worse because there is a question of how I got to the beginning of my run in the first place: this, too, would require an infinite number of steps. Any action, mathematically construed, may seem impossible to complete or even (given that the first step is also mathematically decomposable into an infinite number of divisions) to start.

Mathematicians think that they have a mathematical answer to this paradox: the fractions get smaller and smaller as I approach the bus and so I pass through them more quickly. The successive steps add up to what they call a convergent series. This will not, however, solve the problem because, as philosopher Peter Cave has pointed out, to converge on a goal is not to reach it. The only answer to the question 'How on earth can I catch a bus?' (or, indeed, complete any action) is to reject the premises of the problem and deny that real actions are composed of fractions in the way that Zeno conceived of them: they are not to be understood mathematically. Mathematical steps are not footsteps. If they were, every distance would be the same distance because it would be divisible into an infinite number of elements. To walk is not a mathematical exercise. If it were, then walking would be indeed impossible as it could involve an infinity of steps. But walking *is* possible; and so mathematics is not the way to describe walking. The obstacles lie within maths – or what mathematics has to say about reality – not within walkers. And, indeed, maths does not match, permit, or license actual events. As we have seen from the frozen structures of fundamental physics, mathematics is not at ease with actuality; with the singular reality of events that actually occur at particular times and places. Mathematical entities such as fractions are the eternal, virtual or imaginary, inhabitants of a frozen world.

The perils of what we might call mathematical literalism, which fails to recognise how reality eludes the grasp of mathematics, may be illustrated by an even simpler example. Mathematics deals with lines and their lengths. The world is full of real objects with edges. Lines and lengths never quite match edges.

Consider Bernard Mandelbrot's famous question: how long is the coast of England? There is no definite answer because the result of measurement will depend on the scale used. If you use a theodolite, then you will get one result. If you use a 12-inch ruler that follows all the ins and outs of the coastline, you will get another, much bigger, answer. If you use a micrometer, that is faithful to the bumps on individual pebbles, you will arrive at yet another, much larger, answer. The edges of objects are not mathematical lines (however wriggly) with definite lengths. Indeed, at a certain resolution, even ordinary objects have an indefinite length in that there are clouds of elementary particles emitted from them: they have no more length than a fog has edges.

Of course, from the point of view of the realm of pure quantities unpacked in science, it makes perfect sense to say of one object that it is twice as long as another. But that is an approximation: using the same method, we can say of X that it is twice as long as Y. The approximations cancel out. From the standpoint of mathematics, lines are entirely intelligible and are therefore real, whereas the edges of real objects do not have (pure) mathematical standing.

This is reflected in the continuation of the passage where Galileo asserted that the book of nature was written in the language of mathematics: 'its characters are triangles, circles, and other geometrical figures, without which it is humanly impossible to understand a single word of it; without these, one is wandering around in a dark labyrinth'. From the standpoint of everyday life, however, the reverse is true. Irregularity is the norm; nothing is perfectly congruent with a circle or a triangle (which is why Plato elevated the latter to a higher place, a Heaven accessed by the intellect).

The mathematisation of what is 'out there' extends

our cognitive grasp, enabling us to operate at the highest level of generality. The success of this approach and the practical and theoretical power of the mathematical account of nature should not, however, be taken to demonstrate that the world in which we find ourselves is itself a mere system of magnitudes. Even less should we follow Mad Max in seeing it as one large mathematical structure. To do so would be a perfect example of what the philosopher Alfred North Whitehead called 'the muddle of *importing the mere procedures of thought into the facts of nature*'. The 'procedures of thought' require us to leave much out. Which justifies what the great mathematician and philosopher Bertrand Russell (*Outline of Philosophy*) observed:

We know nothing about the intrinsic quality of physical events except when these are mental events that we directly experience. Physics is mathematical not because we know so much about the physical world but because we know so little.

Behind this assertion is an acknowledgement that mathematical descriptions are profoundly simplifying: there is no set of equations or theorems that can match the complexity of a flower, even less the meadow in which it grows. And the more general the equations or theorems are, the more they endeavour to encompass the totality of things, the more the world they purport to portray is emptied. Fundamental theories in physics reveal only the (abstract) structure or the form of an otherwise unobservable world and not its actual nature.

It would be absurd and deeply ungrateful not to acknowledge the huge contribution mathematics has made to our understanding of the world. Gratitude, however, does not oblige us to adopt a Pythagorean notion that the world is fundamentally composed of mathematical objects such that the whole, fundamental truth about it is captured in the mathematical models developed in advanced physics; that the universe is isomorphic to a mathematical construction.

Mathematics helps us to understand, summarise, predict and manipulate a world whose material does not, however, consist of mathematical objects or structured mathematically. This should be evident from the fact that while mathematically we can multiply time by itself to get t^2 or divide it by space to arrive at velocity this is hardly something that really happens. Try multiplying an actual hour of your life by itself or by another hour. No real stretch of time such as a sunny afternoon – even less a Bargain Break Weekend – would tolerate such treatment.

If time lies beyond the reach of mathematics, the time of our lives most certainly does.

6

– God and Eternity for Infidels –

A while back I was invited by members of the Ahmadiyya Muslim Community to debate whether humanism could replace religion. The courteous tone of the invitation and the reassurance that I was not being teed up as a sacrificial lamb made me inclined to say yes. The website address of the Community – *www.love for all hatred for none.org* – made the invitation irresistible. I therefore accepted, arrived on the appointed day, and spoke my piece. My interlocutor (an Imam) spoke his. We debated with (or talked past) each other and with the very large audience. And that was that. From the 90-minute film of the event (and watching it makes me wish that I looked at my script less and at my audience more) it is evident that, though our exchanges were entirely civilised, we came no nearer to closing the gap between my answer (Yes) and his answer (No).

Even so, putting together my thoughts was a valuable exercise. I discovered that my position (not fully reflected in my speech) was more complex than the straight Yes the dichotomising debate solicited from me. For sure, humanism is not able to replace what religion *promises*. On the other hand, religion does not deliver on those promises, notwithstanding the blood, sweat, toil, tears and treasure it has extracted from human beings who have had, for the most part, little of these to spare. The most significant promises are that there is an all-merciful, all-wise, all-powerful Being who somehow cares what you do and even takes an interest in your welfare; and, secondly, that you have an immortal soul and if you look after it, it will provide a ticket to eternal life. The former speaks to the mystery of our existence and to a lesser extent the tragedy; the latter glances at the mystery but takes the tragedy head on. They are not to be dismissed lightly. Indeed, it is the central challenge of humanism to live without them while not forgetting what lies within us that has inspired them.

Let me begin with the idea of God, as it is evident in the one tradition with which I have the least brushing acquaintance – the Supreme, Ultimate, Personal God of the Abrahamic religions. Given that He has attracted so many believers and at such cost, a humanist who respects humanity must entertain the possibility of His existence.

The appeal to factual evidence is always going to be inconclusive, because there is no general agreement as to what might count as evidence. Miracles, scriptures, the testimony of priests and prophets and so on can all be contested. But for some believers the mere fact that we communicate with one another, or that the world is ordered, or that there is something rather than nothing, is proof of a Creator who not only made the world but also made it habitable by, and intelligible to, us. The absence of evidence is even to be anticipated, since we would not expect God to have local manifestations. Besides, existentially worthwhile belief should be a matter of faith. Yet others have claimed that the burden of proof rests with equal weight on theists and atheists, and that atheists have as much to prove or demonstrate as theists.

Philosopher William Lane Craig is one of the most eloquent and thoughtful of God's recent defenders and his reasons focus on the mystery of our existence. In a recent article ('Does God Exist?') that I came across as the result of the accident that I write for the same magazine, he offered no less than eight reasons for believing in God's existence. Six of them took this form: 'God is the best explanation of . . .' According to Craig, God explains:

1) why there is something rather than nothing;

2) the origin of the universe;

3) the applicability of mathematics to the physical world;

4) the fine-tuning of the universe for intelligent life;

5) intentional states of consciousness – the fact that conscious experiences are about items other than themselves;

6) objective moral values and duties.

Impressive or what?

Some of these reasons are more clearly vulnerable than others. For example, the very idea of (presumably universal) 'objective moral values and duties' is contestable and has prompted not only much verbiage but prejudice, bigotry, oppression, tyranny and frequent bloodbaths. The barbarism of confessional wars shows the dismal failure of a putative God to uphold or at least clearly to communicate universal values. Angry atheists have pointed out that, far from supplying the basis for morality, God has not only behaved amorally (according to his most widely read Fanzine the Bible) but has inspired or licensed or mandated dreadful behaviour (torture, murder, oppression, war crimes etc.) in his subjects. So much for 'objective moral values and duties'.

What about 'God' as a metaphysical explain-all? Consider Craig's first reason: 'God is the best explanation of why anything at all exists'.

His argument (which continues a tradition of many centuries) goes as follows:

1) Every contingent thing has an explanation of its existence.

2) If the universe has an explanation of its existence, that explanation is a transcendent personal being.

3) The universe is a contingent thing.

4) Therefore, the universe has an explanation of its existence.

5) Therefore, the explanation of the universe is a transcendent, personal being.

All three premises are suspect. Take Premise 1. In what sense do we have a (complete) explanation of any particular item? Premise 3 seems odd: Is the universe 'a thing', contingent or not? While there may be partial explanations of individual items, it does not follow that there must be an explanation of the sum total of all things, even less a single, one word, explanation of them ('God'), less still when that word ('God') carries so much historical baggage. You might (in some sense) explain the existence of an item such as Raymond Tallis by referring to other items – his parents – but you cannot generalise this to the sum total of all items. The idea of parenthood – or more generally of a cause – cannot be extended to the totality of Being within which parenthood, or causation, operates. Causes are incorrigibly local – and like the causes that produced Raymond Tallis – they require a vast quantity of supporting conditions.

Explanation operates within Something and cannot expect to have much traction in the Nothing that precedes it, assuaging our perplexity as to why there is anything at all. Explanations – for example 'there was thunder because there was lightning' – only link a bit of Something with another bit of Something. Outside of Something, there is no explanation – least of all an explanation of why there is Something to explain. A satisfactory explanation of Item X by Item Y does not imply that there is a chain of explanation that will extend backwards until we arrive at something (e.g. God) that requires no explanation. Any explanation of the totality of things would have to appeal to something outside that totality, which is surely a contradiction. (This applies with equal force to scientific attempts to explain how Something grew out of Nothing, as we shall see in a minute.)

What about the *character* of this Being called God? Craig slips from God as a necessary 'explanation of existence' to 'a transcendent personal being' (Premise 2) which is crucial to the promise of religion. While this gets him closer to his particular target – the Christian God – it is even more wobbly than Premise 1. When we think of causes we don't think of anything personal. Causes in the universe, with the exception of those late arrivals human agents, tend to be the impersonal effects of other impersonal causes.

Craig tries to justify the transition to a transcendent personal being – the biggest challenge for many theists – by saying this is what everyone means by 'God'. But that's not true: for some, God is impersonal; and for others God is immanent or even without specifiable properties as in the case of the 'apophatic' God. But it's also irrelevant: the epidemiology of belief is not a secure guide to the nature of reality and that which brought it into being. The reason why there is something rather than nothing, or the character of the force that brought it about, is not solved by an opinion poll.

Once the Creator is ascribed any definite characteristics, additional to those directly relevant to His delivering a Something out of Nothing, a new set of troubles breaks out. Referring all explanation back to 'God' takes us to an entity whose nature can be argued over until the cows come home or eternity's sunset. In reality, to use the word 'God' is simply to mobilise a verbal placeholder to fill gaps in our understanding, an office it discharges very badly as it is riddled with conceptual incoherence, and open to a variety of unsatisfactory interpretations.

Craig offers an additional reason for God's existence. It takes a different form and draws on one of the most venerable arguments in the Western theological tradition: the Ontological Argument – updated by recent philosophers. He employs it to arrive at the conclusion that the very *possibility* of God's existence implies that He exists. The argument goes as follows: if 'a maximally great being (God)' exists in a possible world, it exists in every possible world, otherwise it would not be a maximally great being; from which it follows that it necessarily exists in an actual world, in our world.

The idea that God can be imported into our picture of the world via a cunning definition belongs to the wilder shores of scholasticism. The key moves are: a) identifying 'maximally great being' with 'God'; b) asserting without further evidence or argument that if such a being exists it *must* exist; and c) then dropping the 'if'.

Most atheists could rehearse these counter-arguments in their sleep. On the principle of belt and braces, therefore, Craig, like many theologians, supplements his arguments with what he believes to be directly experienced *evidence* that 'God can be personally known and experienced'. Indeed, he worries that 'there's a danger that philosophical arguments for God could actually distract your attention from God Himself'. The emphasis on experience brings us rather neatly to another defence of theism – by philosopher Timothy Chappell in an article twinned with Craig's ('Theism, History and Experience'). Theists, he says, should not be impressed by *arguments* for or against the existence of God. We should focus on *experiences* because experiences cannot be denied.

Chappell offers an analogy. Clever philosophers, he says, are able to demonstrate (at least to their own satisfaction) that there is no incontrovertible evidence for the existence of an external world. We might find these sceptical arguments interesting and even impossible to refute. Even so, we would not for a moment believe their conclusions: our *experience* tells us otherwise. While it is possible, Chappell says, to demonstrate that we cannot know with absolute certainty whether there is an outside world, even to the point of being uncertain as to whether or not we have hands, experience trumps argument.

There are several reasons for dismissing this variation on the (quite popular) appeal to the primacy of experience over argument in support of the existence of God. The most obvious is that while there are many people who sincerely deny the existence of God, particularly the kind of personal God that both Craig and Chappell believe in, no-one could doubt the existence of the outside world or indeed could function if they sincerely did. There have been long periods in history – indeed most of history before the Christian era – when people managed without belief in a single, personal God, an Infinite Intimate who is also the founder and creator of the cosmic order. By contrast, there could not have been periods when people *really* doubted that there was anything outside of their own minds. If there were, we would presumably have no record of them. What would be the point of declaring to a non-existent world that it does not exist? Arguments for denying the reality of an outside world are self-refuting, since they presuppose the existence of other people, and an outside world to house them. The reality of other people, of a community of speakers, is implicit in the very language we use to discuss this matter. How could 'outside' and 'world' have any meaning in a universe confined to the mind of one individual, so that their existence could be denied? It is therefore entirely reasonable to reject the idea that there is no external world, however brilliant the arguments for it. On the other hand, ignoring the arguments against a Personal God – if they are sound – and retreating to an appeal to experience is not reasonable.

So relegating the unbeliever's arguments to mere

'interesting puzzles' that are trumped by theists' *experiences* is not an option, particularly since characterisations of God have the habit of being self-contradictory – to this infidel the key reason for being an atheist. The most discussed contradiction is that an All-Powerful All-Good God is incompatible with the actual world of injustice, suffering and tragedy. Much more telling, however, is the impossibility of entertaining the idea of a personal God who is both infinite and yet transcends His creation or who is simultaneously everywhere and timeless and yet makes specific interventions at a particular place and time.

Responding to the fact that *all* descriptions of God so far on offer are riddled with such contradictions by claiming that something will turn up – or it's just beyond our understanding – is simply another promise. It's certainly not an adequate response to counter evidence of logical inconsistency in ideas of God.

The last ditch defence of theism – the assertion of the primacy of experience over arguments – does not cut much ice since what is at issue is not whether or not theists have certain experiences they regard as revelations of God but the solidity of their grounds for interpreting them in that way. No experience, however subjectively compelling, could of itself provide evidence for the (presumably) objective assertion that there is One (Infinite but Intimate) God. The dodginess of translating personal experience into irrefutable justification of a particular belief about the universe as a whole is betrayed by the fact that other people, with experiences just as profound, have quite different religious beliefs. At any rate, it seems rather vulnerable (to put it mildly) to unpack something as gigantic as the Creator or Cause of the Totality of Things from something as transient and small as a personal experience. The relevant experience can carry authority only if it is already assumed what the experience is to prove; namely that it has been implanted in us by God.

So much for the first promise of religion – a God Who cares for you. What of the second: eternal life?

ETERNITY

The English are not a very spiritual people, so they
invented cricket to give them an idea of eternity.
– attributed to George Bernard Shaw

It wouldn't surprise me if quite a few people are sick of Raymond Tallis but your essayist can't get enough of himself. He consequently finds the thought of his own extinction very uncongenial. Nevertheless, I cannot ignore the lengthening contrail of yesterdays, warning me that my store of tomorrows is depleting. Sometimes I feel like a paddleless canoeist being swept towards a cataract. It becomes more difficult to do without the promise of an indefinitely prolonged afterlife –

compared with which my lost childhood, vanished maturity, and forgotten dotage would be a triad of eye-blinks – and the hope that the tragic mystery of our lives is not tragic after all.

Eternity has a respectable philosophical as well as religious ancestry. It has haunted Western philosophical thought almost from the beginning. We have only to think of Plato's conception of an unchanging Heaven where reality – palely and confusedly imaged in the temporal world experienced through our senses – is present in uncontaminated perfection as those Forms or Ideas glimpsed by the philosophically trained intellect. Eternity is timeless duration. In subsequent millennia, however, the idea of eternity has become rather complicated, contested, and politicised – not least as a weapon in the struggle to maintain the *status quo* in societies where justice is severely rationed. The promise of an Eternal Reward for colluding in your own oppression or the oppression of others takes the pressure off the demand for a living wage, basic rights, or freedom from mistreatment.

But enough of infidel tub-thumping. Let's look at the *concept* of eternity in its purest form. According to the Cambridge philosopher J. M. E. McTaggart, it has at least three facets:

1) An unending stretch of time – everlastingness;

2) that which is entirely timeless;

3) that which includes time but somehow also transcends it.

Everlastingness is eternity's unique selling point. 'Forever and ever' (preferably without 'Amen') is what most of us would want from eternity, notwithstanding there is something not altogether attractive about being allocated an infinite number of days. Suppose they all turned out to be Mondays? And wouldn't we sooner or later run out of things to do, or even to complain about?

Let us turn our attention therefore to the idea of eternity as timelessness. McTaggart distinguished 'the timelessness of truths' from 'the timelessness of existences'. This was a good move, as the qualification for being a timeless truth can be quite unimpressive. While the sciatica I had in 2010 lasted only a few months, the humble truth of the assertion 'Raymond Tallis had an attack of sciatica in 2010' is eternal. That may be why, beginning with Plato, the emphasis has been on timeless existences rather than timeless truths.

Such existences are usually reserved for ontological toffs. For Plato, Ideas or Forms such as Love, the Beautiful, and the Good were Eternity's primary denizens. He couldn't, however, entirely exclude embarrassing ontological proles, such as hair and dirt, without being inconsistent. Platonist mathematicians – who (as we saw in 'All Is Number') believe that their discipline unveils timeless realities – have populated eternity with menageries of mathematical objects such as The Circle, and the Square, integers, and more exotic beasts like pi or the square root of -1. And – most relevant to our present concerns – theologians have peopled eternity with the immortal souls of those who have lived sufficiently blameless lives. Which brings me to the promise of the annulment, or at least mitigation, of tragedy through the idea of eternal life. As with a God who cares for you, there is a problem of delivery on promises.

Considering what happens to our bodies after our demise, resurrection of their flesh doesn't seem on the cards. The laws of nature would seem unlikely to reconstitute their masterpiece (your essayist) out of the confetti of his scattered ashes or reconstruct his once-smiling face from the faeces of creatures who have feasted on his deliquescent visage.

In a discarnate, indeed disembodied, state, he would not be anywhere in particular, and thus not available to impinge or to be impinged upon. Bodiless, he would be without specific needs, desires, hopes or dreams. Consequently, no imaginable action would be necessary or meaningful even if it were possible. Continuation of life under such circumstances would be comparable to breathing in a vacuum. His condition would be more impoverished, at any rate, than a state of frozen expectation, or waiting-for-nothing, since waiting has at the very least the idea of a particular future built into it.

None of which should be grounds for surprise: timelessness must imply changelessness since change cannot occur without time. Anything that really happens occurs at a definite time and takes a definite time. The idea of *life* without change is even more problematic. All forms of living matter – plankton, trees, and your next door neighbour – are in states of constant alteration, corrected by other alterations. This is the 'polyphasic dynamic equilibrium' that is organic existence. Directly and indirectly seeking the right kinds of alterations to head off the wrong ones is the fundamental story of any life. So life in a timeless realm doesn't promise to be exactly action-packed: it would be effectively lifeless. Whiling away eternity would be a trial, particularly if you consider the neighbours you might have. Frozen humans would be bad enough but think of sharing a garden fence with the Form of Good or the square root of minus 1.

McTaggart's third aspect of eternity as something that 'includes time but somehow also transcends it' raises further problems. How can time and eternity connect? Mrs Smith, after a virtuous, god-fearing life, dies in 2015, fully qualified to be fast-tracked to an eternal reward. Assuming that her papers are in order, she arrives in the timeless zone the very day she dies. By 2017, we seem entitled to say that she has spent two years in said timeless zone. But this is manifestly self-contradictory: there can be no years without time. And how can we say of Mrs Smith's 'crossing over to the other side' that it took place *after* her life was finished and *before* her (equally saintly) husband who died in 2019 joined her? What could possibly connect a particular point in time with timeless eternity, without the latter somehow losing its timelessness?

The relationship between time and eternity – or between your essayists' days and the after-Tallis he is contemplating – is clearly a vexed one. It causes especial difficulties for theologians when they try to make sense of eternity's star inhabitant – God – popping out to make interventions in historical time, for example, smiting those who have made Him wrathful. (Is God's irritability due to a particularly severe form of jet lag resulting not from crossing time zones but from crossing into and out of the zone of time itself?) The difficulty of His intervening at a particular point in history is compounded if we think of God the way that Boethius conceived him in *The Consolation of Philosophy*. Boethius' God was eternal and eternity for Him was 'the simultaneous and perfect possession of everlasting life' embracing 'the whole of everlasting life in one simultaneous present'. It must be difficult to dismount from this simultaneous totality to get on with the mucky business of stacking the odds against the Canaanites or giving the Philistines what for.

It is easy to mock theologians if one forgets that their difficulties are analogous to those which face physicists trying to accommodate the fact that particular events happen, actually take place. Physics imagines a world shaped by general laws. Indeed, as physics advances, so the laws get more general. Unfortunately, general laws don't deliver singular events; indeed, the more general they are the less they deliver. No wonder the space-time manifold of Relativity Theory – in which everything is present at once and unchanging – seems to be as frozen as the eternity of theologians, though God's eye view has been replaced by the virtual view-from-nowhere of glass-eyed mathematics.

Perhaps the most beautiful expression of the vexed relationship between time and eternity is to be found in this famous passage in Plato's *Timaeus*:

Wherefore he [God] resolved to have a moving image of eternity, and when he set in order the heavens, he made this image eternal but moving according to number, while eternity itself rests in unity; and this image we call time.

Time as 'the moving image of eternity' is certainly beautiful; but it is also baffling, and remains so even if we accept the dubious idea that time is something that is on the move. The 'moving image' of something that is fundamentally unmoving would seem like a misrepresentation to which a God should not be party.

The intersection between time and eternity generates not only paradoxes but also ironies. They exercised the second most famous melancholy Dane: the great ironist Soren Kierkegaard. In *Either/Or* he talked about 'the aesthetics of marriage' where the partner, showing fidelity to eternal vows in a temporal and temporary life, is able to solve 'the great riddle of living in eternity and hearing the hall clock strike'. At any rate ordinary believers must sometimes wonder about the church clock making them hurry so as not to be late for Mass and miss an appointment with the Eternal Being, as if the Eucharist were a booked meal.

The existential and logical impossibilities that seem to discredit the idea of eternity may make us feel that it is a term to which nothing corresponds, a mere shadow cast by language. We may think that 'eternity' stands simply for a non-existent opposite of all that is transient; that the idea of the time*less* is parasitic on the notion of time. In short, that (to borrow from St John) 'In the Beginning was the Word'. However, we can't, on this basis, dismiss the term as merely empty. For we are in the vicinity of a very profound mystery.

All beings – stones, beetles and people – are (in some almost impossible to specify sense) *in* time. Only one has the *idea* of time. Man is the being for whom time, uniquely, is explicit: he *times* time, translating the apparent movement of the sun into hours on the clock, months on the calendar. He alone has placed inverted commas around it and called it 'time'. Even infidels like myself must therefore acknowledge this mysterious background whence the notion of eternity – unending time, timelessness, or a container that transcends and encloses time – has emerged. It raises questions about what kinds of beings we are, where we fit into the order of things; more specifically whether, after all, we are so fundamentally different from other creatures that a different fate may await us when our hearts stop beating and our supply of tomorrows gives out. These may seem dangerously heretical thoughts for an infidel but the very existence of the idea of eternity keeps the door of its possibility ajar. However, it does not seem to palliate the tragedy of our transience.

So while – to answer the question posed by Ahmadiyya Muslim Community – humanism may seem to be unable to replace religion because it does not promise a personal God to take an interest in your welfare or an eternal life to offset the transience of this one, religion seems unlikely to deliver on these promises if only because they appear unintelligible.

THE MYSTERY AND THE TRAGEDY

We have to come to terms with a life that is a sometimes joyful and sometimes tragic mystery. The joy is contingent, the tragedy inevitable. Religion furnishes its believers with the promise of something to address both the mystery and the tragedy but delivery falls short. Does humanism have anything to replace this?

First, the mystery. It has many storeys. Humanists have no idea why there is Something rather than Nothing. We do not know how living creatures arose in a small part of this something. And we are quite unable to explain the emergence of consciousness (even less a self-consciousness such as yours and mine) in a tiny proportion of those living creatures. Of course, there are some individuals who believe that we have such explanations or are *en route* to them.

Lawrence Krauss, for example, thinks he knows how the universe arose from nothing, thus fulfilling the famous promise made by John Tyndall in 1874 that men of science would 'wrest from theology, the entire domain of cosmological theory'. The universe, cosmologists tell us, grew out of a false vacuum: a quantum field or 'inflaton' which was temporarily stable but not in the lowest energy state. Random fluctuation (uncaused, as things are in the quantum world) sent the inflaton tumbling into a true vacuum. This generated an equal amount of positive energy (matter) and negative energy (gravity) which adds up to nothing: the total mass energy of all the constituents of a finite universe is equal in magnitude but opposite in sign to the total gravitational potential energies of those particles. So the universe could be created from Nothing because it adds up to Nothing. The Big Bang, which blasted the Universe, Being itself, into being, was simply a rearrangement of Nothing. We now know with extraordinary precision when Nothing learned to punch above its weight by becoming two opposite kinds of Something: between 13.77 and 13.78 billion years ago. What's more (we are told) we can trace the exact details of the conjuring trick as far back as the first 10^{-30} seconds.

Notwithstanding this fancy footwork, it is obvious that cosmology does *not* deliver on the promise to render the Creation stories of theologians redundant. An 'unstable quantum vacuum' in the starter pack is a bit more than Nothing. Jitteriness requires more than Nothing to host it, whatever the paradoxes of quantum mechanics permit. And the idea that we can finesse a Universe from Nothing, while still respecting the law of the conservation of energy by a process that generates equal amounts of positive and negative energy so that the universe has zero total energy, seems to be somewhat literal-minded. It takes the pluses and minuses in an equation for reality. If the signs really were real, and they added up to nothing, we would have to think of gravity as not merely nothing but *less than nothing*. Less than nothing would find it hard to keep itself going.

It is difficult to see how this could make anything other than mathematical sense and we know from 'All is Number' how far 'mathematical sense' does (or does not take) us. It certainly cannot deliver the kind of sense required to translate mathematical equations into an empirical description, explanation, or account of a world in which actual particular events occur. And equally unexplained are the *laws* that are supposed already to be in place to ensure that instabilities in the quantum field unfold into a universe. Can we conceive of laws being allowed to anticipate, and hence exist independently of, a universe in which they will operate; that, for example, the laws of gravity could exist in the absence of actual gravitational fields to regulate?

What's more, given that the Big Bang is a singular event – or at least so far as this universe goes – it seems strange to think that it can be explained by (general) laws captured in mathematics.

As a result of wresting the question of the origin of the universe from theologians, and replacing a Creator with self-creating physical phenomena, cosmologists seem to have turned one unanswerable question – Why is there something rather than nothing? – into at least three: How did the quantum vacuum arise to kick-start everything? How did it generate two kinds of Something – unpacked into a positive and a negative universe? And How come there were already laws of nature to guide it? The mathematico-physical demonstration that there is (a net) Nothing to explain does not seem like an explanation when there is manifestly plenty to explain, notably that there is Something after all. Replacing the Creator by a creative accountant who somehow gets the bottom line to zero does not seem like a great advance.

And that's just the first question. What of the origin of life? If we start from physics, we face a huge obstacle in explaining the availability of the most basic constituents of living matter, such as carbon. The odds of the fundamental constants of the emergent universe – the masses of fundamental particles and the strengths of their mutual interactions – having by chance the values necessary to make stable carbon atoms are unimaginably small. Desperate situations require desperate remedies. None is more desperate than the idea (based on a particular interpretation of quantum mechanics) that there are vast numbers of parallel universes hidden from us, together instantiating the entire range of possible values for the basic constants. By this means, the odds of carbon appearing by chance are greatly reduced. If you buy enough lottery tickets, you can make the jackpot a dead cert. Since these universes are not accessible to observation, however, this seems less a scientific theory than a *post hoc* rescue job, even though it is also motivated by the need to deal with some of the more egregious aspects of quantum weirdness.

The theories concocted to address the origin of the universe and its apparent fine-tuning to make life possible have precipitated something of a crisis in leading edge physics, as I mentioned in the previous essay 'All Is Number'. But there are more unanswered and (seemingly unanswerable) questions in the queue. How did carbon and nitrogen and other key elements meet to form self-replicating molecules such as DNA? How did DNA eventually situate itself in (*take a deep breath*) highly structured cells with a multitude of complex components working together in harmony, enclosed in a membrane facilitating the entry of desirable materials, excluding undesirable ones and excreting what should be excreted, and equipped with exquisitely folded internal membranes that bring together that which needs to interact and keeping other things apart? If we can't answer these questions, we have no idea of the substrate upon which natural selection can operate to transform random variation into the driver for evolution towards increasing complexity. The more we learn about cells – and the dense networks of regulated actions and interactions taking place within them and within their packed organelles and microtubules and other semi-permeable membranes – the more distant seems the goal of understanding how they work as a whole. And analogous problems arise at higher levels. How systems and organs – ranging from bacteria with their waving flagella to kidneys, hearts and brain – could arise and work both alone and in conjunction with other organs and systems remains unclear.

Bullish atheist biologists (BABs) deny that the complexity of living systems is irreducible and argue that such complexity will sooner or later be fully explained by the operation of natural selection on spontaneous variations in simpler organisms. Wiser or more honest heads know that we cannot even begin to envisage how innumerable traits work together in the whole that is the organism. BABs fear that candour about the difficulties of getting from molecules to cells to organs will be exploited by evangelical salesmen flogging the empty doctrine of Intelligent Design, according to which an intelligent process, rather than something undirected such as natural selection, is driving the emergence of increasingly complex forms of life. Of course, like full-blown Creationism – the appeal to

God the Creator as an explain-all – Intelligent Design is no explanation at all. But the BAB denial of the difficulties does not alter the facts that we do not have an explanation of the origin of even microscopic life nor a sure path to such an explanation.

As for consciousness, it, too, is mysterious at many levels. Why it should arise – what distinct purpose it serves – is utterly baffling to anyone who questions the usual assumption that awareness might give an organism an edge over the competition. After all, unconscious mechanisms are good enough to direct the behaviour of most living organisms, and are perfectly adequate for the spectacular task of constructing a human foetus or the brain that is the necessary condition of consciousness. By definition, mechanisms driven by natural laws – unlike choices informed by sentience – are utterly reliable. And mechanisms totally innocent of consciousness have shaped the most cunning strategies in the various arms races between predators and the preyed upon.

Equally unclear is how consciousness, even if it really did confer distinct advantages, might arise in a universe that is presumed to be overwhelmingly insentient and has been entirely without consciousness for all but a tiny part of its existence. The intractability of the problem is highlighted by the fact that the relationship between activity in the brain and conscious experiences, felt emotions, memories, intentions and so on, is incomprehensible. Nearly all neural activity, even in the human brain, is not associated with any conscious experience. Nerve impulses in the spinal cord, cerebellum, brain stem, deep hemisphere structures, and most of the cortex, look very like those in the supposed centres of consciousness and (to anticipate the usual argument) the 'wiring' in the latter is also very similar to that seen in the parts of the brain that are without consciousness. Not that it is easy to see how the way the neural wires are connected could account for the profound difference between the parts of the brain that are, and those that are not, aware of the world around them.

And then there is person-hood – I-hood, you-hood, essayist-hood. The sustained sense of self, supported by memories that reach into a personal past and by expectations that light up an imagined future that is 'my' future where explicit goals are located, are even less amenable to explanation by neural activity than sentience or basic experience. Consider just one aspect of this: the unity of moment to moment consciousness. Our moments are experienced as being composed of a multitude of distinct experiences and thoughts and memories. This cannot be explained by neurones converging on a single spot tying the contents together because those contents would then lose their distinct identity in the merged or summed activity from different sources. The multitudinous components of moments are experienced, or are available to be attended to, separately – that is why I am able to refer to them now. This unity-and-multiplicity of my 'nows' makes the mysterious three-in-one of the Trinity seem comparatively simple.

LIFE WITHOUT RELIGION

So there we have it: the multi-storied mystery of the Universe, of Life, and of Us. Though science falls far short of providing anything approximating explanation, this does not justify appeal to a Divine Maker. A mystery – even a unique or many-layered one – does not make the case for God, even less one that is imagined and worshipped in any particular religion. 'God' invoked in this context would simply be a placeholder, or a place-blocker, pre-empting any search for explanation rather than counting as an explanation. But a humanism that would replace religion must keep the mystery alive; explicitly live within it; even entertain the possibility that we, like iron filings unaware of the magnetic field, or stones not experiencing our gaze, might fall within a consciousness higher than our own.

This is easier said than done. Without the support of the structures, rituals, and obligations of organised religion, not to speak of their threats and promises, the mystery of our lives has to struggle to find its place in competition with compelling priorities. For many human beings, indeed probably most of us over history, *the* over-riding concern has been survival, getting enough to eat and drink, making a living, and dealing with the threats – to life, limb, liberty, comfort, and dignity – originating from the natural and human world. Even those who are not pinned to the ground by destitution, or by a hostile material and social environment, are usually exercised by the pursuit of prosperity, of status, and riches. The breathing spaces opened up by relative affluence, and the automated support structures for everyday living, are often occupied by new needs that can be multiplied without limit, by all-absorbing desires, fulfilled and unfulfilled, preoccupations with getting and spending, with one's standing, by fears large and small, shame and embarrassment, envy, jealousy, and an endless supply of recreations, pastimes, and less structured distractions. More worthy of praise are the distractions of responsibilities, duties, our sense of what we owe to others, that direct our gaze to a multitude of tasks, projects large and small, preparations and reflections, the construction and dismantling of what we and others have built. Densely woven, multidimensional networks of 'in-order-tos' fill our days, taking us to goals that we do not quite reach even when they are achieved: arrival at a destination turns out to be another piece of *en route.*

For all of these reasons, the *mysterium tremendum* of our life and the universe in which it is lived, that figures so largely in the religious discourse if not often in the lives of believers, is a minor presence. We have an unlimited capacity for forgetfulness and shallowness.

The mystery of existence seems to be an optional concern, displaced as easily by the desire to show off or realising that one has lost one's wallet, as by unhappy love or the symptoms of a fatal illness.

While we have to reach out to the mystery of life, its tragedy, by contrast, sooner or later reaches out to engulf us. Joy is precarious and fleeting, the contingent child of a convergence of happy accidents, while tragedy is the permanent condition of our existence. That ultimate predator – the transience and finitude of all things – is inescapable: the processes that made us will sooner or later unmake us, whatever steps we take to postpone disintegration. We will lose everything that we have loved, everything that we have earned, possessed, and built, and most especially, we will lose ourselves. There is no such thing as a long life, only degrees of brevity.

This, then, is the challenge for believers and infidels alike: to awaken out of the sleep of normal wakefulness to a deeper and more continuous awareness of the fundamental truth of our condition. A life that is lived in the presence of the mystery and the tragedy of things would seem to have a true coherence, a fidelity to itself, rising above a mere torrent of events, experiences, plans, crises, distractions endured and sought out: it would be a life characterised by that 'purity of heart' which is 'to will one thing' that Soren Kierkegaard spoke of as his ideal.

Since such an ideal is honoured in devotion to a

God and in the hope of an eternal afterlife, is there anything in it that secular humanists can draw upon? The very fact that God and Eternity are human (indeed all-too-human) constructions should give pause to a humanist, though this is often given as an even more compelling reason for setting them aside than any putative damage they have caused. Even if God were, as Diderot expressed so brilliantly in his parable, the most terrible and incomprehensible idea mankind has ever entertained, it is also the most profound. It straddles life and death. It has sufficient draft – to use a nautical term –to be adequate to the existential reality of our tragic condition, reminding us of our nakedness and vulnerability in an inexplicable, enchanting, cruel, and wonderful world. 'God', what is more, is the ultimate expression of our capacity to entertain possibility, which includes the possibility of things that do not, or could not exist. It is a place where our (uniquely human) sense of all that is hidden from our collective understanding comes together. Elusive, unimaginable, self-contradictory, the idea of God – in which the beliefs of each are supported by the beliefs of all, corks lifted on the sea of faith – is as deep as the bonds that tie us to society of which, according to many thinkers, God is a displaced image.

Spanning life and death, respecting the mystery and tragedy of our condition, God and eternity import a weight of meaning proportionate to the gravity of our circumstances, and offer a place of convergence for all the sources of significance in our lives, linking the details that detain us with the large facts that contain us, hinting at an understanding in which scientific truth, human meanings, and our purposes, metaphysics and morality, find a common origin and destination. We infidels need something comparable to what is asserted or presupposed in religious rituals to counter the elusiveness and brevity of lives framed by the twin forevers of our non-existence.

While secularisation has brought huge benefits, liberating lives and minds, the project of finding something to fill the emptiness left in the wake of religion has taken humanity into some dark places. By a hideous irony, this has sometimes been particularly evident in lives where a sense of purpose is sought and found in the idea of service to others. The hideous consequences of finding a substitute for the consolations and legitimations of institutionalised religious belief through the top-down transformation of secular life were first seen clearly in the state-sponsored savageries of the French Revolution.

Just how far the wish to give greater meaning to one's life through devotion to an ideal can be corrupted both individually and collectively was demonstrated by the catastrophic secular religions of the 20th century, in which the greater good was defined by 'Dear Leaders', 'Great Helmsmen', 'Fathers of the Nation' supported by a priestly caste of privileged interpreters, privileged bureaucrats ruling by the document and the sword, Party grandees who were the equivalent of the prelates of the Church. As has often been pointed out, totalitarian states and their ideologies replicated the pattern of abuse seen in religious institutions. The Devil finds work for idle churches. Religions – with or without God – are after all as much about belonging as about belief, defined by criteria for exclusion and inclusion, for the right to membership of the Church or the Party. In the secular religions, solidarity, ruthlessness towards heretics, often rooted primarily in the desire for self-advancement or even the need for survival, triumphed over justice, decency, kindness, and any commitment to finding or telling the truth. The commitment of idealists was exploited by ambitious scoundrels appropriating the rhetoric of a higher calling to acquire an unassailable, absolute authority. The brutal pursuit and exercise of power perverted the dream of universal emancipation, material advancement, and justice that were the stated aims of these secular religions. And they exploited the hope of a way of life where the tragedy of finitude could be mitigated by devotion to the creation of an Earthly Paradise that seemed more solid than any of the traditional ones already established in Heaven.

What the worst aspects of various brands of Communism and all of Fascism had in common with the religions of salvation that preceded them was that, at their heart, there was an alliance with death. Religion valued the afterlife over this one; Fascism glorified death in war; and Communism (in theory at least) privileged the inhabitants of the distant future over the expendable present generation.

The millenarian and the totalitarian converge at so many points, not least in the terrible ironies of the distance between the radiant theory and hideous practice. What Albert Camus referred to as 'slave camps under the flag of freedom' mirror the torture and blood baths of religious wars waged to promote the teachings of the Prince of Peace. In the ever-receding future of the earthly Paradise promised by totalitarian regimes, a future for the sake of which nothing or no-one should be spared, the prospect of choirs of angels and a pleased deity is replaced by the expected gratitude of generations to come. In this respect, as in so many others, these secular religions are deeply anti-humanist.

CODA:

INFIDELS AWAKE! SALUTE THE HAPPY MORN

The provision of transcendental, and hence unchallengeable, justification for the establishment and maintenance of political power based on hatreds old and new, might seem a warning to humanism to distance itself from religious modes of thought. Even so, there is, as Philip Larkin wrote, something that 'never can be obsolete':

Since someone will forever be surprising
A hunger in himself to be more serious
  – 'Churchgoing'

A hunger, that is, that the ideas of God and eternity seem uniquely to address; a seriousness without which life is in danger of becoming two-dimensional.

Taking humanity seriously therefore includes engaging with the undelivered hopes and promises of religion; reflecting on what our religious past and present says about us and on the extraordinary truth that for much of history humans have lived their lives in the light and darkness of ideas to which, according to humanism, nothing corresponds. What kind of creatures are we that are able to create such wonderful works and perform such terrible deeds at the prompting of a God that does not exist? And, more to the point, what kind of future can we make for ourselves when we are free of this notion but do not wish to lose the profundity from which it grew?

A passage from an ex-Christian Diarmid MacCulloch in his *Christianity: The First Three Thousand Years* is particularly pertinent:

I still appreciate the seriousness which a religious mentality brings to the mystery and misery of human existence, and I appreciate the solemnity of religious liturgy as a way of confronting these problems.

I, too, embrace the seriousness, the solemnity and the intuitions of mystery and joy – and the buildings and the art, the music, the poetry, the novels, the drama, the painting, that have been inspired by the idea of God or a God-haunted world – while firmly setting aside much of the rest, most notably the arrogant, divisive, and inflammatory claims to revealed truth.

At any rate, humanism needs to engage more closely with religion than certain scorched earth atheists would wish. This is not a case for flinging oneself at the foot of the Cross, worshipping Allah, putting on a skull cap in the presence of Jehovah, or going even further afield in the shopping mall of theological ideas. In short, for dipping into what Philip Larkin called 'the myth kitty'. Only for accepting that a humanism that is truly mindful of religion and what it has meant may be less prone to the arrogance and ignorance that leads some thinkers to overlook the unfathomable mysteries in which we are immersed, and as a result to fall under the spell of a disenchanted naturalism that overlooks the transcendence in our shared humanity. The exemplar of certain religious modes of understanding in which meanings converge should inspire us to try harder to become equal in thought to the reality of our condition and of the world in which we live our largely inexplicable lives; to unlock the self-forg'd manacles of habit; to acknowledge the mystery of human life without siding with its tragedy.

Art liberated from servitude to religion, to patrons,

and propaganda, is a natural ally. Aesthetic experiences are, however, rarely integrated into more coherent and continuous mode of feeling, thinking, and acting, and sometimes break down into a succession of episodes. Our hunger for more seriousness asks for something more.

The challenge of humanism is to retain a numinous sensibility without the continuing support of the idea of God or churches, to cultivate a sense of possibility that goes beyond the apparent givens of the world we erroneously think we know too well; to find a way of living or at least imagining life to the full in the absence of the undelivered and undeliverable promises of religion; to be as profound in atheism as theists are, or were, in their experience of God and the expectation of an afterlife.

This is what I really should have said when I addressed the members of the Ahmadiyya Muslim Community but it really wasn't the place. I hope the reader will forgive this extended instance of *l'esprit d'escalier.*

Other titles from Notting Hill Editions*

A Short History of Power
by Simon Heffer

Taking a panoramic view from the days of Thucydides to the
present, Heffer analyses the motive forces behind the pursuit
of power, and explains in a beautiful argument why history is
destined to repeat itself.

On Dolls
edited by Kenneth Gross

The essays in this collection explore the seriousness of play and
the mysteries of inanimate life – the 'unknown spaces, dust, lost
objects, and small animals that fill any house'. *On Dolls* includes
contributions from Baudelaire, Rilke, Freud, Elizabeth Bishop
and Marina Warner.

On the Natural History of Destruction
by W. G. Sebald

In the last years of the Second World War, a million tonnes
of bombs were dropped by the Allies on 131 Germans towns
and cities. Sebald's classic essay explores the consequences for
the German people, and his bafflement at German collective
amnesia.

Confessions of a Heretic
by Roger Scruton

A provocative selection of essays by the influential social
commentator. Each 'confession' reveals aspects of the author's
thinking that his critics would probably have advised him to
keep to himself.

'Scruton is ne of the few intellectually authoritative voices in
modern British conservatism.' – *The Spectator*

CLASSIC COLLECTION

The Classic Collection brings together the finest essayists of the past, introduced by contemporary writers.

Grumbling at Large – Selected Essays of J. B. Priestley
Introduced by Valerie Grove

Beautiful and Impossible Things
– Selected Essays of Oscar Wilde
Introduced by Gyles Brandreth

Words of Fire – Selected Essays of Ahad Ha'am
Introduced by Brian Klug

Essays on the Self – Selected Essays of Virginia Woolf
Introduced by Joanna Kavenna

All That is Worth Remembering
– Selected Essays of William Hazlitt
Introduced by Duncan Wu

*All NHE titles are available in the UK, and some titles are available in the rest of the world. For more information, please visit www.nottinghilleditions.com.

A selection of our titles are distributed in the US and Canada by New York Review Books. For more information on available titles, please visit www.nyrb.com.